RATIONAL EXPECTATIONS

Rational Expectations, Non-market Clearing, and Investment Theory

MARK PRECIOUS

CLARENDON PRESS · OXFORD

1987

Oxford University Press, Walton Street, Oxford OX2 6DP

Oxford New York Toronto
Delhi Bombay Calcutta Madras Karachi
Petaling Jaya Singapore Hong Kong Tokyo
Nairobi Dar es Salaam Cape Town
Melbourne Auckland
and associated companies in
Beirut Berlin Ibadan Nicosia

Oxford is a trade mark of Oxford University Press

Published in the United States
by Oxford University Press, New York

British Library Cataloguing in Publication Data
Precious, Mark
Rational expectations, non-market
clearing, and investment theory.
1. Investments
I. Title
332.6'01   HG4515
ISBN 0–19–877256–4
ISBN 0–19–877255–6 Pbk

Library of Congress Cataloging in Publication Data
Precious, Mark.
Rational expectations, non-market clearing,
and investment theory.
Bibliography: p. Includes index.
1. Investment analysis. 2. Rational expectations
(Economic theory) 3. Equilibrium (Economics) I. Title.
HG4529.P74 1987   332.6   87–1552
ISBN 0–19–877256–4
ISBN 0–19–877255–6 (pbk.)

Phototypeset by Macmillan India Ltd.
Printed in Great Britain
at the University Printing House, Oxford
by David Stanford
Printer to the University

Preface

Investment theory is interesting not only because it is a crucial macroeconomic variable, but also because its proper analysis forces one to confront the central problems of economic theory: namely, how do economic agents form their expectations, and how do they behave in a world where markets may not always work as smoothly as introductory books tell us?

This book provides a comprehensive analysis of firms' investment behaviour. To do this existing work is summarized, from Keynes to Tobin's 'q' theory, and it is shown how these models can be extended and combined in a way which, it is hoped, both clarifies previous work and presents new insights.

As the title suggests, however, the intended scope of the book is wider than a presentation of investment theory. The methodology employed aims to fit investment models more cohesively within the two main developments of macroeconomic theory during the last decade: namely, the rational expectations theory and the disequilibrium or non-market-clearing theory. The two approaches are combined to produce a general intertemporal theory of the firm in a world where markets may not clear. In this way I hope the student will understand more not only about the investment, output, and employment decisions of such firms, but also about the approaches themselves.

This book should be of use to both undergraduates and postgraduates. I have tried to make a sometimes complex subject both simpler and readable. Wherever possible, I have simplified the mathematical content of the analysis. It is not possible to avoid mathematics altogether, but there is no reason why an interested reader should not able to master all the techniques used. There are two main 'tricks' used which an undergraduate may find new: the first is the use of phase diagrams, the second is intertemporal optimization. Both are explained in detail. The rest is algebra.

Finally, I would like to thank the many people who have contributed to the appearance of this book. I am particularly grateful to John Flemming, Jeremy Edwards, David Begg, and Colin Mayer for all their help and encouragement, and to Marcus Miller and George Yarrow for making me believe that my findings warranted publication. I owe a special thanks too to Andrew Schuller of OUP for his patient allowances for numerous broken deadlines. Lastly, and most importantly, I would like to thank my wife Amanda for all her moral support and practical assistance in getting the manuscript to the publishers in a readable form.

Contents

Contents

Introduction

The subject of this book is investment theory examined in the light of the two major developments in recent macroeconomics: namely, rational expectations theory and disequilibrium theory. The aim is twofold. First, though occupying a central position in macroeconomic theory, rational expectations theory and disequilibrium theory have pursued largely divergent paths. This independent development has been highlighted in the sometimes acrimonious debate between Keynesians and monetarists over macroeconomic policy formulation.

The New Classical Macroeconomics, using the assumption of rational expectations, argued that demand management policies will have little effect on real variables even in the short run. Orthodox Keynesians continued to argue otherwise.

One resolution to this debate which explains the different results is that, for the conclusions of the New Classical Macroeconomics to hold, rational expectations theorists had also to make the additional assumption that markets continuously clear. In non-market-clearing models Keynesian policy results remained valid. However, while this was true, the models of the disequilibrium school, for example Barro and Grossman (1971) and Malinvaud (1977), were largely atemporal and hence neglected the important question of expectations. Clearly, for general results there is a need to combine rational expectations and non-market-clearing theories, and this book represents one such attempt in the field of investment theory.

Second, investment theory itself is not uncontroversial and has produced a large number of apparently independent and often contradictory models. However, while the developments in dis-equilibrium theory have shown the importance of correctly specifying the market conditions in which agents operate for understanding the general theory of unemployment, it seems the same lessons have not been absorbed in investment theory. Seen in this light, the postwar literature on investment has two major shortcomings. (1) It has focused almost exclusively on the demand side of the market. Thus, consideration is given to the factors affecting a firm's demand for new investment goods while little is given to the implications for aggregate investment of the behaviour of the capital-goods-supplying industry. (2) Despite the concentration on the demand side of the investment process, there has been no general analysis of the implications for investment of the different market conditions in which demanding firms operate.

My second aim is therefore to remedy these shortcomings: first, by examining the implication of taking account of supply-side considerations for both Jorgenson's neoclassical theory and 'q' theory, the two strands that have dominated the investment literature over the last two decades; and second, by providing a generalization of neoclassical 'q' theory to take account of disequilibrium in both the goods and the labour market and so providing a unified analysis of the firm's investment decision in a variety of different market conditions.

That so little attention should have been focused on the supply side of the market is surprising when one notes that such a generalized framework does exist. We need only go back to the *General Theory* to see that Keynes explicitly refers to the importance of the effect of a rising supply price of capital goods, as investment demand increases, upon the determination of actual investment.

Chapter 1 covers the background by looking at the main developments in the investment literature to date. The accelerator, neoclassical, putty–clay, adjustment cost, and 'q' theories are all summarized and analysed. In the above list there is of course the major omission of Keynes. In Chapter 2, therefore, we shall look closely at Keynes's theory of investment. We shall examine the importance Keynes assigned to the capital-goods-producing industry in determining actual investment and explain his idiosyncratic views on the way entrepreneurs form their expectations as summarized by the term 'animal spirits'. Animal spirits play a crucial role in Keynes's theory of investment. I take the work of Witte (1963) as a representative example of previous expositions of the Keynesian theory of investment and argue that he, in common with other authors, commits a general methodological error which I go on to correct in Chapter 3.

There I extend the work of Marshall, Sampson, and Sedgwick (1975), which incorporates an upward-sloping supply function for new capital goods into the standard neoclassical framework of Jorgenson, to produce a consistent representation of Keynes, capable of reflecting the volatility of expectations expressed by 'animal spirits' and the influence of supply factors on actual investment. The model also allows an interesting re-examination of the original work of

Jorgenson and the precise role of a putty–putty technology in influencing investment.

In his later work, Jorgenson (1972) argued for the inclusion of the assumption of adjustment costs in the analysis of investment. The assumption of increasing marginal costs of adjustment implies a determinate rate of investment in the neoclassical model. Firms therefore must react to anticipated future changes. In Chapter 4, building on the work of Abel (1979), I look at the relationship between Keynes, Tobin's 'q' theory and the neoclassical investment theory of Jorgenson, extended to include adjustment costs. I also for the first time introduce the theme that will occupy us for the remaining chapters of the book, namely, the analysis of investment behaviour when firms recognize the possibility that markets may not clear. It is in this chapter therefore, that we first see the synthesis of rational expectations and disequilibrium theory. Specifically, in Chapter 4 I extend the result of Hayashi (1982) to show the relationship between average and marginal 'q', and therefore between stock market value and investment demand, when markets do not clear.

Chapters 5, 6, 7, and 8 continue with this framework to present a 'q' model of investment extended to take account of disequilibrium in the goods and labour markets. The use of phase diagrams allows a diagrammatic representation of the full dynamic behaviour of such firms. Specifically, I look at the demand or sales constraints (Chapters 5 and 6), employment constraints (Chapter 5), and investment constraints (Chapters 7 and 8). As well as a model of investment, the analysis gives us a powerful, general intertemporal model of the firm which may be rationed in different markets.

In the sphere of investment, it provides a unified analysis of the traditionally independent cost minimization and profit maximization approaches to investment theory, allows for the possibility of 'regime-switching', as in Malinvaud (1977), and allows us to re-examine properly the old issue of the investment response of firms to demand and relative prices. In Chapter 7, the model provides a general analysis of investment constraints, including as a special case the problem of the irreversibility of investment, studied by Arrow (1968) and Nickell (1974a, 1974b). Finally, in Chapter 8 I look at the effects of different assumptions about supply-side behaviour upon the relationship between investment, 'q', and capital goods prices.

1

Postwar Theories of Investment

1 Introduction

The postwar literature on investment was dominated originally by the accelerator theories of investment and more recently by the neoclassical theory originated by Jorgenson and the 'q' theory suggested by Tobin. The links between these theories have often been difficult, if not impossible, to see, in part because they lack a common framework. In this chapter I shall explain outstanding features of these theories, together with their various offshoots, such as adjustment cost and putty–clay models of investment; and in working through their underlying assumptions I shall try to show the distinctions and similarities between them.

2 The Accelerator Theory of Investment

I shall begin, in chronological order, with the accelerator theory of investment. The simplest form of the model is known as the 'naïve accelerator' and states that investment is determined by the current change in output; that is, if K_t, Q_t are the capital stock and output respectively of the firm at the time t,

$$K_t - K_{t-1} = v\,(Q_t - Q_{t-1}) \tag{1}$$

or

$$\Delta K_t = v\,\Delta Q_t \tag{2}$$

where Δ stands for the change in K, Q between one period and the next, and v is a constant which tells us what fraction of the change in production is translated into investment. When early investment models of this type were tested empirically, a slightly more complex version of the theory, known as the 'flexible accelerator', was found to perform much better. This says that investment is still determined essentially by demand and output, but that the feed–through from changes in production might not be as simple and direct as envisaged in the naïve accelerator model. The flexible accelerator says that

$$I_t = K_t - K_{t-1} = v\lambda \Delta Q_t + v\lambda(1-\lambda)\Delta Q_{t-1}$$
$$+ v\lambda(1-\lambda)^2 \Delta Q_{t-2} + \dots \quad (3)$$

or

$$\Delta K_t = v\lambda \sum_{i=0} (1-\lambda)^i \Delta Q_{t-i}. \quad (4)$$

This equation says that (net) investment, ΔK_t, is no longer determined just by current changes in output, but also by earlier changes in output. There are at least two possible explanations for this. The first is that, for some reason, the firm can adjust only gradually, rather than instantaneously, to changes in demand. Thus, the firm will increase part of its capital stock today in response to a change in output, and will go on reacting to that change of output over time. We can therefore introduce a distinction between the firm's actual and desired capital stock, K_t and K_t^*, respectively. Assume that desired capital stock K_t^* depends solely upon output: $K_t^* = vQ_t$, and therefore $\Delta K_t^* = v\Delta Q_t$. Thus, desired investment is related to current changes in output. In other words, the firm would *like* to react instantaneously to changes in output (as it implicitly does in the naive accelerator); however, it may be subject to delays owing to, say, lags in the delivery of the investment goods, which means that in practice it can do only a fraction of the desired investment; that is,

$$\Delta K_t = \lambda(K_t^* - K_{t-1}). \quad (5)$$

Equation (5) says that actual investment ΔK_t is only a fraction λ of the desired investment, measured by the difference between the firm's capital stock at the end of the previous period and the desired capital stock for this period. Now, substituting for K_t^* from above, we get

$$K_t - K_{t-1} = v\lambda Q_t - \lambda K_{t-1}$$

or

$$K_t = \lambda v Q_t + (1-\lambda)K_{t-1}.$$

But, in the same way, $K_{t-1} = \lambda v Q_{t-1} + (1-\lambda)K_{t-2}$, and so, by simple substitution,

$$K_t = \lambda v Q_t + (1-\lambda)\lambda v Q_{t-1} + (1-\lambda)^2 \lambda v Q_{t-2} + \dots$$

and so,

$$\Delta K_t = \lambda v \Delta Q_t + \lambda v(1-\lambda)\Delta Q_{t-1} + \lambda v(1-\lambda)^2 \Delta Q_{t-2} + \ldots$$

or

$$\Delta K_t = \lambda v \Sigma (1-\lambda)^i \Delta Q_{t-i} \tag{6}$$

which says that investment is a weighted average of past changes in output, where, since λ and $(1-\lambda)$ are fractions, the importance of any given change in output upon current investment declines through time.

The second explanation of the flexible accelerator model focuses on expectations. Suppose firms form their expectations of future output/demand, on which they then base their investment decisions, by looking at current and past levels of demand. Current investment will then be a weighted average of current and past change in output, as shown by the following simple example. Assume that the firm remains optimally adjusted so that actual and desired investment are equal, but that desired capital stock depends upon expected output at time t. Put another way,

$$K_t = K_t^* = vQ_t^e.$$

Therefore,

$$\Delta K_t = \Delta K_t^* = v\Delta Q_t^e = v(Q_t^e - Q_{t-1}^e). \tag{7}$$

If entrepreneurs have adaptive expectations, then

$$Q_t^e - Q_{t-1}^e = \lambda(Q_{t-1} - Q_{t-1}^e). \tag{8}$$

In words, entrepreneurs adjust their expectations by a fraction of the extent to which they guessed wrong—actual output did not equal expected output—in the previous period. Simple manipulation of (8) shows that

$$Q_t^e = \lambda Q_{t-1} + \lambda(1-\lambda)Q_{t-2} + \lambda(1-\lambda)^2 Q_{t-3} + \ldots \tag{9}$$

and hence expectation of output at time t is a weighted average of previous levels of output. Substituting (9) above, we get

$$\Delta K_t = v\Delta Q_t^e = \lambda v \sum_{i=0} (1-\lambda)^i \Delta Q_{t-i-1} \tag{10}$$

which again gives us the flexible accelerator formulation.

The possibility arises, therefore, that an investment equation may 'perform' well in empirical work and seem to provide a good explanation of the data, but that the underlying reason for this remains unclear: in this case, do firms form their expectations adaptively, are there delivery lags, or is it a mixture of both?

A good deal of the remainder of this book looks closely at the progression from one investment model to another and hence at those assumptions that are common to the different theories and those that separate them. In general, however, as we shall see, at an empirical level there has been considerable difficulty and controversy in establishing the precise role of different factors in the investment process.

The same problem arises when we consider the underlying technology of the firm that is assumed under the accelerator theory of investment. As we have seen, the distinguishing feature of accelerator theories is the emphasis upon demand or output as the determining factor in investment. Relative prices (interest rates, wages, input prices), and hence profitability, seem to play no explicit role. We shall return to this question in looking at the neoclassical theory of investment, but for the time being let us assume that firms suffer some form of demand constraints and therefore cannot sell their desired output. Firms will therefore choose their inputs—capital and labour, say—and hence make their investment decisions in order to minimize the cost of producing a given level of output. Clearly, then, output or demand is crucial variable in determining investment, as the accelerator theory predicts. Nevertheless, the prices of the inputs available to the firm should still affect both the quantity and the type of investment it makes. Why do these variables not enter into the equation? What else is there that underlies the theory?

The first explanation lies in terms of technology. If the firm's production possibilities are described by a fixed-coefficients production function, then for a cost-minimizing firm the optimal capital stock will be uniquely determined by output. Figure 1.1 illustrates a

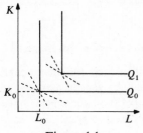

Figure 1.1

fixed-coefficients technology. The two right-angled lines illustrate the quantities of capital and labour needed to produce the levels of output Q_0 and Q_1. The right-angled shape implies that, in the production of Q_0, the most efficient choice of capital and labour, *regardless of relative prices*, is K_0 and L_0, respectively. No further output is produced, even if more labour is added, if capital remains fixed at K_0. Similarly, increasing capital yields no extra output if the quantity of labour is fixed at L_0. Thus, whatever relative prices are, there is a unique optimum level of capital (and labour) needed to produce each output level. If we also assume constant returns to scale (CRS), the naive accelerator model follows.

The second explanation allows capital to be substituted for labour in the production of a given level of output, so that the isoquants may be smoothly curved, as in Figure 1.2. In this case relative prices are important. The firm, as before, chooses the cheapest combination of capital and labour to produce a given level of output, but this now changes as relative prices change. Hence there will in general be no unique relation between desired capital and output. However, *if relative prices remain constant*, and if there are constant returns to scale, it should be clear that a naive accelerator result will again follow.

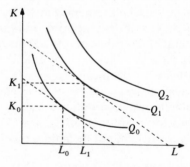

Figure 1.2

3   The Neoclassical Theory of Investment

In 1963 a paper published by Jorgenson challenged the accelerator theories of investment. Jorgenson assumes a textbook neoclassical world of perfect competition where firms have perfect foresight and face given current and future prices. Just as in static models, profit maximization yields the optimal values of labour and output, so in this intertemporal model, optimizing behaviour by firms gives the optimal values of the capital stock and quantity of labour employed at each point in time, and from this Jorgenson derives an investment equation.

Jorgenson assumes a decreasing-returns-to-scale production function $Q = F(K, L)$, where capital and labour can be smoothly and continuously substituted as in Figure 1.2. The assumption of perfect competition applies to all markets, including the capital market (where the firm can therefore borrow and lend as much as it wants at the given rate of interest) and the second-hand capital goods market. It also assumes that there are no costs involved in either the sale or the purchase of investment goods or the installation of capital. Finally, although taxes can be introduced into the model, for simplicity we shall ignore them in what follows.

What will an optimizing firm do? First, as in the static model, the firm will always produce output and adjust its labour force until the marginal product of labour equals the real wage—in other words, until the marginal cost of another unit of labour equals the marginal benefit, or

$$\partial Q/\partial L = F_L(\cdot) = w/p \tag{11}$$

Where w = wage rate and p = price of output. But, since there are no costs to adjusting capital, exactly the same argument applies to the capital stock. The firm will go on adjusting its capital stock until the marginal cost of another unit of capital is equal to the marginal benefit, that, is, until

$$\frac{\partial Q}{\partial K} = F_K(\cdot) = \frac{c}{p} = \frac{q(r+\delta) - \dot{q}}{p} \tag{12}$$

where q = price of investment goods, δ = rate of depreciation, r = interest rate, and $\dot{q}$ = rate of change of price of capital goods.

What does the expression on the right-hand side of (12), called by some the 'user', or 'rental', cost of capital, mean? Just as the wage rate is the cost of hiring a unit of labour for one unit of time, so, too, c is the cost of hiring a unit of capital for one unit of time. It is made up of three components:

1. the interest cost of a machine valued at q;
2. the depreciation cost as a fraction δ of the machine is used up during the time it is used;
3. the capital gain or loss on the machine during the period.

The cost faced by the firm, whether implicit (if the firm has actually bought the machine) or explicit (if the firm has rented the machine), will be the same, since with perfect markets the firm will be indifferent between renting and buying the machine. It is, however, probably easiest to think of a firm that buys the machine and holds it for one period.

Since the Jorgenson model can at first sight be somewhat bewildering, it is worth taking time to show that his first-order condition, equation (12), is no more than the more familiar present value condition. This is most easily done if we switch to a discrete-time formulation of the equation, which is

$$p_{t+1} F_{K(t+1)} = q_t(1+r) - q_{t+1}(1-\delta).$$

Rearranging this gives

$$q_t = \frac{p_{t+1} F_{K(t+1)}}{1+r} + q_{t+1} \frac{(1-\delta)}{1+r}. \tag{13}$$

In words, firms should go on buying capital goods until the purchase price is equal to the discounted marginal benefits given by the revenue obtained from the machine that becomes available at the beginning of the next period plus the discounted value of that part of the machine remaining at the end of the period. This is therefore a present value condition for a firm that can dispose of capital assets at the end of each period. By continuous substitution for q, the equation assumes the even more familiar form:

$$q_t = \frac{p_{t+1} F_{K(t+1)}}{1+r} + p_{t+2} F_{K(t+2)} \frac{(1-\delta)}{(1+r)^2}$$
$$+ p_{t+3} F_{K(t+3)} \frac{(1-\delta)^2}{(1+r)^3} + \ldots .$$

That is,

$$q_t = \sum_{i=1}^{\infty} \frac{p_{t+i} F_{K(t+i)}}{(1+r)} \left(\frac{1-\delta}{1+r} \right)^i \tag{14}$$

which says that in the Jorgenson world the firm invests until the cost of the machine is equal to the discounted marginal revenues from the output of the machine. The move from (12) to the more recognizable but equivalent forms of (13) and (14) also demonstrates what we said above: namely, that the Jorgenson firm is indifferent between renting the machine period by period and buying the machine and holding on to it.[1]

In the Jorgenson world, with perfect competition, perfect foresight, and no costs of adjustment, the firm adjusts instantaneously to changes in its economic environment. It is therefore always optimally adjusted. In deriving an investment function, this presents a potential problem. Since investment is the rate of change of the capital stock, a firm that responds instantaneously to, say, a change in the rate of interest has an infinite rate of investment and hence the investment function would be undefined.

Jorgenson sidesteps this problem by ruling out discrete instantaneous changes in the capital stock in response to, say, a change in the rate of interest. This he can do because of special assumptions he makes about the pattern of price adjustment. He assumes that 'forward prices or discounted future prices of both investment goods and capital services are left unchanged by variations in the rate of interest'. This is as follows. If the unexpected change in the rate of interest occurs at t_0, the Jorgenson adjustment process is that $\dot{q}(t_0)$ accommodates the change in r, leaving the cost of capital, which is

$$c(t_0) = q(t_0)\{r + \delta - \dot{q}(t_0)/q(t_0)\},$$

unchanged. With $q(t_0)$, $c(t_0)$ constant, this implies, from the definition of $c(\cdot)$, that future capital goods prices will be lower. And, because $(r + \delta - \dot{q}/q)$ is, by assumption, unchanged by variations in the rate of interest for all future t, this implies that future c will also be lower than otherwise. To maintain the equilibrium condition $F_K(t) = c(t)$, firms will therefore desire higher capital stocks, implying a higher rate of investment. By comparison of such alternative paths for the capital stock (known as comparative dynamic analysis), we can conclude that investment is inversely related to the rate of interest.

Three points have been emphasized with regard to Jorgenson's neoclassical model. First, it was the first investment function rigorously derived from an optimization model of the firm where all assumptions were clearly spelt out. It was a pioneering piece of work which dominated the investment literature for more than a decade, and its importance can be gauged by the extent to which later writers have either produced refinements of the basic theory or, in seeking to change the direction of investment theory, have taken the neoclassical model as their starting point.

Second, the first-order condition describing firms' optimal behaviour is a 'myopic' one. In other words, despite the fact that Jorgenson sets up a fully intertemporal optimizing problem with firms maximizing profits through time and looking ahead at future variables, the equation

$$[\partial Q/\partial K = F_K(\cdot) = q\,(r+\delta) - \dot{q}]$$

contains only current variables. Authors have therefore argued that the Jorgenson investment model is not truly intertemporal, since technically the firm does *not* require information about the future time paths of input and output prices. It simply maximizes in the usual static fashion at each instant of time t. This, it is argued, is a result of the assumptions on the technology and the assumption that there are no costs of adjustment. Capital goods today are identical to those tomorrow (and yesterday). If a firm buys capital goods and uses them, then a fraction of these goods (δ each period) depreciates, but what is left is exactly the same qualitatively as the goods it bought at the beginning of the period, and indeed as the new goods it can buy now. In addition, since there are no costs of adjustment, and perfect markets, the firm can costlessly buy and sell whatever quantity of capital goods it wants. If it has too much capital at the end of the period, it costlessly offloads it on to the perfect second-hand goods market at a known price. And vice versa, if the firm has too little capital.

This is correct and is an unrealistic feature of the original Jorgenson model, which arises because it has no explanation of how the prices of capital goods are determined. There is no separate capital-goods-producing industry, and hence no supply side to the model which can be used to define the path of capital goods prices. Prices are therefore simply given exogenously to demanding firms rather than being determined within the model. In a more realistic model, with the supply side included, expected future changes *do* affect firms' future profitability and hence their future demand for capital. With limited capacity on the supply side of the industry, this affects future and current capital goods prices, and the myopic behaviour of firms disappears. The absence of any focus on the supply side of the investment model is not a criticism unique to Jorgenson. It applies to the majority of theories since Keynes, and is an important theme to which we shall return in Chapters 2 and 3, when we look at Keynes's theory of investment and an extended neoclassical model of investment with a capital-goods-producing industry included.

Third, in contrast to the accelerator theories, the neoclassical theory emphasizes relative prices, interest rates, and tax variables as important influences upon the firms' investment. The reason for this we already know. With a technology in which capital can be substituted for labour in the production of output, the firm will choose its capital and labour so as to minimize the cost of producing any given level of output. Hence anything that affects the relative price of labour and capital will influence firms' investment. It is clearly vital for policy-makers to know whether it is relative prices or demand that influences investment, since on this depends the appropriate choice of government policy to stimulate investment. We therefore now turn to the empirical implementation of Jorgenson's work, about which there has been considerable controversy. First, what does Jorgenson do to develop an empirically testable investment equation? He assumes a specific functional form for the production function, the Cobb–Douglas $Q = A K^{\alpha} L^{\beta}$ with $\alpha + \beta < 1$, which implies decreasing returns to scale. With this production function, the marginal product of capital $\partial Q / \partial K = \alpha(Q/K)$, and so the first-order condition for the neoclassical model becomes

$$\frac{\partial Q}{\partial K} = F_K(\cdot) = \frac{c_t}{p_t} \Rightarrow \alpha \frac{Q_t}{K_t} = \frac{c_t}{p_t} \Rightarrow K_t^* = \frac{\alpha p_t Q_t}{c_t}.$$

Therefore

$$\Delta K_t^* = \alpha \Delta \left(\frac{pQ}{c} \right)_t. \tag{15}$$

Jorgenson now adds the assumption that there are delivery lags for the new capital goods, with the result that only a fixed fraction λ_0 of the goods ordered this period are actually delivered, a fraction λ_1 of the orders of this period are delivered next period, and so on. So actual investment in any period t is made up of the fraction of the goods ordered and delivered in period t plus the deliveries of investment goods made this period but ordered earlier; that is,

$$I_t = \Delta K_t = \lambda_0 \Delta K_t^* + \lambda_1 \Delta K_{t-1}^* + \lambda_2 \Delta K_{t-2}^* + \ldots \text{ (etc.)}.$$

Therefore

$$I_t = \lambda_0 \alpha \Delta \left(\frac{pQ}{c} \right)_t + \lambda_1 \alpha \Delta \left(\frac{pQ}{c} \right)_{t-1} + \lambda_2 \alpha \Delta \left(\frac{pQ}{c} \right)_{t-2} + \ldots.$$

$$= \alpha \sum_{i=0} \lambda_i \Delta \left(\frac{pQ}{c} \right)_{t-i}. \tag{16}$$

This is the basic form of the equation estimated by Jorgenson. Unfortunately, there are substantial objections to this procedure. First, Jorgenson's maintained hypothesis of a Cobb–Douglas production function and his subsequent derivation of the desired capital stock term does not allow a direct test of what he is wanting to prove: that relative prices matter. Since the relative price and output terms enter his estimating equation as a composite term, it is impossible to separate out the influence of output and relative prices on investment. Second, many of the assumptions used in the empirical model are inconsistent with his theoretical work. Therefore, while one might accept or reject the empirical work, this does not imply acceptance or rejection of his theoretical work.

Briefly, with regard to this latter point, there are two contentious areas:

1. the adjustment process of the firm: Jorgenson's theoretical work implies that the firm is always optimally adjusted, yet in his empirical work he imposes an *ad hoc* delivery lag;
2. econometric objections to the empirical work: critics have argued that the methods used by Jorgenson will lead to biased and inconsistent estimates, for example owing to autocorrelated errors and lagged dependent variables (output) on the right-hand side of the equation.

The question of the endogeneity of output in the Jorgenson model is worth pursuing. A perfectly competitive neoclassical firm *chooses* the output it wishes to supply. To have output as an explanatory variable is therefore inconsistent with the use of ordinary least squares (OLS) estimation techniques, since it implies an endogenous variable on the right-hand side of the equation. To avoid this error there are two options, neither of which Jorgenson takes. The first is to solve for desired output, giving an expression for desired capital stock solely in terms of exogenous variables (the prices). This is straightforward to do. There are three equations:

$$Q = AK^\alpha L^\beta$$

$$\frac{\partial Q}{\partial K} = \alpha \frac{Q}{K} = \frac{c}{p}$$

and

$$\frac{\partial Q}{\partial L} = \beta \frac{Q}{L} = \frac{w}{p}$$

and three unknowns, Q, K, L. We can therefore solve the equations giving an expression for K^* in terms of the relative prices w, q, r, p. When estimated this way by, say, Brechling (1975), the neoclassical model performs very badly.

The alternative is to derive the estimating equation by assuming cost minimization by the firm and hence an implicit demand constraint where the level of output is given to the firm. In this case the first-order conditions for the firm reduce to

$$\frac{F_K}{F_L} = \frac{c}{w} = \frac{q(r+\delta) - \dot{q}}{w}. \tag{17}$$

This simply says that a cost-minimizing firm goes to the point of tangency between the isoquant (the slope of which gives the marginal rate of substitution (MRS) between K and L and is measured by F_L/F_K) and the relative price line (see Figure 1.3). c is the price of hiring a unit of capital for one period, w is the price of hiring a unit of labour for one period. At point A it is not possible to substitute capital for labour (or vice versa) and reduce the cost of producing output, Y_0. If we now assume a specific functional form for the production function, an investment equation can be derived which has an exogenous demand term on the right-hand side (see Brechling 1975).

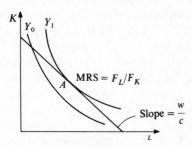

Figure 1.3

4   Putty–Clay Theories of Investment

We have seen that, except in the special case where the neoclassical theory produces an accelerator model (cost minimization, constant returns to scale, and constant relative prices) what distinguishes the two models is the underlying technology. In the accelerator model, a fixed-coefficients production function implies that relative prices do not matter, while the smooth substitution possibilities of the neoclassical production function imply the opposite. We have, however, been too restrictive. There is an intermediate possibility which arises if we make a distinction between the *ex ante* and *ex post* technology available to the firm. It is quite plausible to suppose that the set of possibilities open to a firm when it is choosing the type of machine it wants to buy may well be larger than the corresponding set of possibilities once the machine is constructed and installed. In other words, *ex ante*, the firm may be able to choose from a range of machines of different capital–labour ratios, but *ex post*, when it has chosen and installed the particular machine, it is difficult to alter the capital–labour ratio. To use the terminology of the literature, *ex ante* 'putty' has become *ex post* 'clay'.

In the fixed-coefficients technology ('clay–clay'), there is no factor substitution either *ex post* or *ex ante*. Hence both the *ex post* and *ex ante* isoquants have the right-angled shape we have already seen in Figure 1.1. The neoclassical production function ('putty–putty') allows continuous factor substitution but again assumes that the substitution possibilities are the same *ex post* as *ex ante* (Figure 1.2). It is, as we have seen, a world of fully general-purpose machines which operate effectively at any job. If an investment is made for future expected output and demand for that product falls, the putty is reshaped (at zero cost) and is employed to produce other types of output. Investment is therefore fully reversible.

Putty–clay models of investment differ significantly from the putty–putty and clay–clay models in that the *ex ante* and *ex post* elasticities of substitution are no longer assumed equal. Diagrammatically, this means that the *ex ante* and *ex post* isoquants are no longer identical. *Ex ante* substitution between factors is possible, and the firm can choose the capital–labour ratio it wishes, say, point *A* in Figure 1.4). However, the decision, once made, determines the factor proportion over the remainder of the economic lifetime of the machine.

The economic implications of the putty–clay assumption are important. First, unlike the clay–clay models, relative prices matter. Second, unlike in the original Jorgenson model, expectations play a crucial role in a putty–clay technology. In a putty–putty world, capital equipment can be costlessly reshaped in the next period in accordance with a change in relative prices. In a putty–clay world, by contrast, a

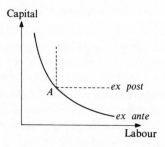

Figure 1.4

real long-term decision exists. Many efficient blueprints exist for new capacity, but the firm must choose the blueprint embodying the optimal capital–labour ratio, and it can do that only by looking at future relative prices. A firm that chooses machines with a low capital–labour ratio will have made a poor choice if wage rates are expected to increase significantly during the lifetime of the machine.

The putty–clay model is thus an intermediate case between the pure neoclassical and accelerator themes, and in some respects is a significant advance on both. Empirical work on the putty–clay model has therefore helped shed light on the debate about the relative importance of demand and relative prices on investment. Summarizing the wealth of conflicting econometric evidence that has been produced on the accelerator/Jorgenson debate, we can say broadly that:

1. an investment equation in which investment depends only on relative prices performs very badly;
2. investment equations that include both relative prices and output terms perform well and provide evidence that relative prices influence investment—indeed, Jorgenson, together with various collaborators, has claimed that they outperform accelerator models;
3. however, this evidence is not always unambiguous or uncontroversial—the former because in the Jorgenson model, as we have seen, output and relative prices are tied together because of the Cobb–Douglas assumption, the latter because there is a dispute about the econometric validity of the results.
4. when the relative price and output terms are separated out by, say, Eisner and Nadiri (1968, 1970), output usually appears to have a

significantly stronger influence upon investment than relative prices.

Putty–clay models carry one further important, testable, implication about the *timing* of the response of investment to changes in relative prices and demand. If the world really is putty–clay, we would expect to see investment react to both relative prices and demand, but we would expect the speed of reaction of investment to be different. To see why, consider the difference for a cost-minimizing firm between an unanticipated increase in demand and a change in relative prices that implies an equal increase in firms'optimal long-run capital stock. In the case of the increase in demand, the firm can react immediately by buying in new machinery. However, for a change in relative prices, the firm must wait until the old machinery becomes economically or physically obsolete before being able to buy in the new machinery embodying the new optimal capital–labour ratio. So, for the cost-minimizing putty–clay firm, we would expect to see a faster reaction of investment to changes in demand than to changes in relative prices.

Evidence in support of differences in timing of the response of investment to demand and relative price changes has been found by Bischoff (1969, 1971b) Eisner and Nadiri (1968) and Hausman (1973). However, while persuasive, this evidence is unfortunately not conclusive, since, as Abel (1981) has shown, the same relative speeds of adjustment can be derived from an intertemporally optimizing firm with a putty–putty production function, if we make the additional assumption of costs of adjustment.[2]

More telling evidence in support of the putty–clay model comes with the impressive empirical work of Hausman (1973), who tests it against both the (accelerator) clay–clay and (Jorgenson) putty–putty models using a common data set, together with a common time period and a common statistical technique. Hausman concludes that the putty–clay model is superior in terms of both goodness of fit and predictive power.

5   Cost of Adjustment Models

Later work of Jorgenson incorporated an assumption of convex costs of adjustment into his neoclassical theory. Adjustment costs are those costs associated with the buying or selling of capital goods over and above the basic price of these goods. The assumption is meant to capture such costs as lost output arising from reorganizing and retraining when new equipment is installed.

The theoretical attraction of the assumption for Jorgenson is that it rules out the possibility of instantaneous adjustment by individual firms. Since adjustment costs are assumed to be increasing at the margin, it is cheaper for firms to spread their investment expenditures over time rather than to do it all immediately. It pays firms to adjust gradually, and a distributed lag formulation for the investment equation can be justified.[3] It also means, by extension, that expectations are again crucial, since, by anticipating future changes, firms can react and gradually adjust their investment expenditures in advance of the change happening, thereby reducing total costs. Very briefly, the optimizing behaviour for a firm subject to costs of adjustment is described by the following equilibrium condition:

$$SP_t + C'(I_t) = DP_t \qquad (18)$$

where $C(I)$ are the adjustment costs, $C'(I)$ are the marginal adjustment costs, DP and SP are the demand and supply prices, respectively. This simply says that an optimizing firm equates the marginal cost of buying an extra machine (which is now no longer just the supply price of the machine but also the marginal adjustment cost) to the demand price or marginal benefit—which in a profit-maximizing model would be the discounted marginal revenue from the machine

$$\sum_{i=0} \frac{p_{t+i} \, F_{K(t+i)}}{1+r} \left(\frac{1-\delta}{1+r} \right)^i$$

and in a cost-minimizing model would be the marginal wage bill savings from the substitution of capital for labour:

$$\sum_{i=0} \frac{w}{1+r} \frac{F_{K(t+i)}}{F_{L(t+i)}} \left(\frac{1-\delta}{1+r} \right)^i$$

We shall look in detail at the implications of such models in Chapter 4 and thereafter, but for the time being we merely anticipate the results by noting that adjustment costs therefore introduce a wedge between the demand and supply price of a machine. And, from (18), the larger the gap between the demand price and the price of the machine, the more the firm will invest, even though this incurs higher costs of adjustment. This is because the larger the gap between the demand and supply price of a capital asset, the greater is the incentive to invest and hence the greater the marginal cost of investment the firm can bear. Even with this preliminary glance at adjustment cost models we can therefore extract the important conclusion that investment is an increasing function of the ratio of the demand to supply price of a capital good.

6 Tobin's 'q' Theory

Finally, we consider the approach of Tobin. As defined by Tobin and Brainard (1977), 'q' is simply the ratio of the market valuation of reproducible real capital assets to the current replacement cost of those assets. If the market value of an asset is higher than the cost of purchasing it, there will be an incentive to invest in that asset. An increase in the market valuation of houses relative to the current cost of building will encourage residential construction. The incentive is the gain to be made by the excess of market price over replacement cost. Tobin and Brainard argue, therefore, that investment is related to 'q' as defined above, which is essentially the ratio of demand to supply price. *Investment is therefore again related to the discrepancy between demand and supply price, as in the adjustment cost models.* In fact, this argument can be made more exact. Abel (1979) showed that the neoclassical investment theory, modified by the assumption of adjustment costs and Tobin's 'q' theory, are equivalent. The argument is straightforward. Let us call the ratio of the stock market value of the firm to the replacement cost of its capital stock, *average* 'q'. Tobin realized that the concept relevant for investment is *marginal* 'q' defined, as above, as the ratio of the market value of new additional investment goods to their replacement cost. Taking capital goods as the numeraire, and therefore setting their price equal to unity, marginal 'q' is simply the demand price, or marginal benefit, of a unit of investment. At the optimum, this will be set equal to the marginal cost which, with strictly convex costs of adjustment, is increasing in the rate of investment. Hence the neoclassical theory augmented by adjustment costs implies a determinate rate of investment which is an increasing function of 'q'.

Typically, however, empirical implementation of Tobin has formulated the theory in terms of the ratio of the stock market value of the firm to the replacement cost of its capital stock, that is, average 'q'. The attraction of this formulation was that it seemed to offer the possibility of empirical tractability, by relying on asset markets to digest all relevant expectations and reflect them in stock market prices. Empirical work therefore only needed to rely on an observable market variable to summarize all the information concerning expectation formation, market conditions, and technology that we have already briefly seen divided the numerous previous formulations of the investment equation. While the formulation of Tobin's theory in terms of average 'q' therefore has clear attractions, and has received some empirical support, we shall see in Chapter 4, when we deal with this question in detail, that there are compelling theoretical reasons for doubting that this is the whole story.

7 Conclusion

I have now introduced the main theories of investment, with the one major exception of Keynes. With the adjustment cost and 'q' theory models I have been deliberately brief, since these models—or, to be more precise, a combination of these models—form the subject matter of Chapters 4–8.

Of the remainder, we have looked at the assumptions underlying the accelerator and neoclassical models, and I have briefly summarized the much debated evidence about the importance of relative prices and demand in influencing investment expenditures. We also looked at the putty–clay theory, an interim case between the original accelerator and neoclassical models, which has greater theoretical plausibility and has received empirical support. It implies that both relative prices and demand are important, and hence that both fiscal measures (such as investment and depreciation allowances, corporate taxation, etc.) and monetary policy, through interest rates, will affect investment along with general macroeconomic policy decisions which influence the level of demand.

I shall now correct my major omission and turn to the investment theory of Keynes, which complements later work by emphasizing the importance of supply factors, something that in this chapter has received only brief and unsatisfactory treatment in the discussion of delivery lags and adjustment costs.

Notes

1. The analogue of this result in continuous time is that the expressions

$$\dot{q}(t) = q(r + \delta) - p(t) F_K(t)$$

and

$$q(t) = \int_t^\infty p(s) F_K(s) \exp\{-(r + \delta)(s - t)\} ds$$

are equivalent. In fact, we get from one to the other by differentiation. Thus, differentiating the expression for $q(t)$ with respect to t, that is,

$$\frac{d\{q(t)\}}{dt} = \frac{d\left[\int_t^\infty p(s) F_K(s) \exp\{-(r+\delta)(s-t)\}ds\right]}{dt},$$

gives

$$\dot{q}(t) = q(t)(r+\delta) - p(t) F_K(t).$$

I introduce this result now because in future chapters we shall work with continuous time and this 'trick' is used repeatedly.

2. We shall look at this question in detail in Chapter 6.
3. We saw in Section 2, that the flexible accelerator leads to a distributed lag formation. Not surprisingly, therefore, it is reasonably straightforward to show that the flexible accelerator model can be derived as an adjustment cost model for an appropriate specification of the technology. See Nickell (1978, 30–1) and Junankar (1972).

2

Keynesian Investment Theory

1 Introduction

A significant element in the theory of investment set out by Keynes in the *General Theory* (1936) is the emphasis on the potential importance of the behaviour of the capital-goods-producing industry as a determinant of investment expenditures. Despite this, the postwar literature on investment, dominated first by the neoclassical theory of Jorgenson and more recently by 'q' theory, has focused almost exclusively on the demand side of the story. Thus, 'q' and the expressions derived by Jorgenson tell of the incentives to invest on the part of *demanding* firms. In the following chapter, therefore, and also in Chapters 7 and 8, we shall examine in some detail the implications for both Jorgenson and 'q' theory of taking account of supply-side considerations. As a prelude to this, though, we shall first look quite closely at Keynes's theory and note that there have nevertheless been a number of attempts in the literature to set forth a Keynesian theory of investment—for example, Haavelmo (1960), Lerner (1944), Witte (1963), and Ackley (1961). This work has not, however, been free of criticism—not least from Jorgenson himself (see Jorgenson 1966). I therefore go on to outline a 'representative' exposition of that work— namely, that of Witte—before looking at the objections to it.

2 Keynes, Investment, and Expectations

The main structure of Keynes's theory of investment is to be found in Chapter 11 of the *General Theory* (Keynes 1936, esp. 135–7). There are two distinctive components. First, as in much of the *General Theory*, Keynes emphasizes the role of expectations, and it is in the theory of investment that we see how entrepreneurial expectations, summarized by the term 'animal spirits', play a crucial role in determining the level of investment and hence aggregate demand. It is also here, and in more detail in Chapter 12, that Keynes sets out his rather idiosyncratic views on expectations and agents' behaviour under uncertainty which show the term 'animal spirits' to be so appropriate. Second, Keynes explicitly refers to the supply price of machines, which suggests that he may have had in mind a two-sector model. One of the reasons given for the downward-sloping marginal efficiency of capital schedule is the inelasticity of supply of the capital-goods-producing industry.

It is helpful to begin by defining the terms used by Keynes. The *prospective yield* of an asset is simply the series of expected net returns from that asset. The *supply price* of a capital asset is straightforwardly 'the price which would just induce a manufacturer newly to produce an additional unit of such assets'. The *marginal efficiency of capital* (MEC) is 'that rate of discount which would make the present value of the series of annuities given by the returns expected from the capital asset during its life just equal to the supply price'. Finally, the *demand price* of an asset is simply its present value where the expected net returns are discounted by the current rate of interest.

Thus, the MEC is a rate of discount, ρ, defined by

$$\sum_{i=0}^{n} \frac{Q_{t+i}}{(I+\rho)^i} = SP_t \tag{1}$$

where $Q_{t+i} \equiv$ expected net returns at time $t+i$;
$SP_t \equiv$ supply price of the asset at time t;
$n \equiv$ the life of the asset.

The demand price at time t, DP_t, is given by

$$DP_t = \sum_{i=0}^{n} \frac{Q_{t+i}}{(I+r)^i} \tag{2}$$

where $r \equiv$ the rate of interest.

Almost invariably, Keynes's theory of investment is now summarized by the equilibrium condition that investment be carried out until the marginal efficiency of capital is equal to the rate of interest. However, there are good reasons for trying to avoid this representation. By use of the MEC concept, Keynes lays himself open to criticisms of the internal rate of return criterion.[1] It is as well to know, therefore, that there is an alternative expression which avoids this fault. Also, as it is stated, this seemingly simple criterion pushes to the background some complexity and so is often better known than understood.

A more useful formulation is in terms of the familiar demand and supply price terms and shows that Keynes's equilibrium condition is simply a discounted present value criterion. To see this, note that, from the earlier definitions (1), (2),

$$\text{when } \rho = r \text{ this implies that } DP_t = SP_t. \tag{3}$$

Not surprisingly, Keynes is well aware of this:

The rate of investment will be pushed to the point on the investment demand schedule where the marginal efficiency of capital in general is equal to the rate of interest. *The same thing can also be expressed as follows.* If 'Q_r' is the prospective yield from an asset at time 'r' and 'd_r' is the present value of £1 deferred 'r' years at the current rate of interest, $\Sigma Q_r d_r$ is the demand price of the investment; and investment will be carried to the point where $\Sigma Q_r d_r$ becomes equal to the supply price of investment as defined above. [Keynes 1936, 137; emphasis added].

Going beyond the equilibrium condition, Keynes argues that 'the prospective yield [of any given type of capital] will fall as the supply of that type of capital is increased' (1936, 136), and so we can write

$$DP^i = DP(n_i, r) \tag{4}$$

where $n_i \equiv$ the quantity of new investment goods of type i purchased by the firm, with $\partial DP(\cdot)/\partial n_i < 0$ from above and $\partial DP(\cdot)/\partial r < 0$, for obvious reasons.

Keynes also argued for an upward-sloping supply price schedule:

If there is increased investment in any given type of capital during any period of time, the marginal efficiency of that type of capital will diminish as the investment in it is increased ... partly because, as a rule, pressure on the facilities for producing that type of capital will cause the supply price to increase. [Keynes 1936, 136]

Thus

$$SP^i = SP(n_i) \tag{5}$$

where $\partial SP(\cdot)/\partial n_i > 0$. The equilibrium condition which therefore summarizes Keynes's theory of investment theory is given by

$$DP(n_i, r) = SP(n_i) \tag{6}$$

which can be solved to give

$$r = L(n_i) \tag{7}$$

relating the rate of interest and the rate of investment.[2] Figure 2.1 illustrates this point.

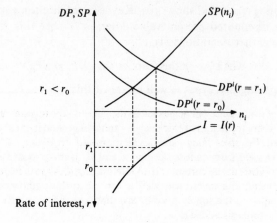

Figure 2.1

The advantage of working in terms of demand and supply price, therefore, is that we can see just how much is going on behind Keynes's investment schedule. In particular, the above makes clear that the investment schedule is a market equilibrium curve derived by tracing out the locus of pairs of points relating the rate of interest to the *equilibrium* level of investment obtained from the intersection of demand and supply price curves. It does not give investment demand for different rates of interest holding all prices constant, as is often assumed. Instead, it gives the actual rate of investment, which in such a market-clearing model will indeed be equal to investment demand but at the changed price of capital goods.

Following on from this, we can see that the effect of taking account of an upward-sloping supply function for new capital goods is a reduced *initial* response of investment to a fall in the rate of interest, and that the response is spread out over several periods rather than there being an instantaneous (one-period) adjustment to the new long-run equilibrium position. This is most easily seen in Figure 2.1 if we assume given supply conditions and zero depreciation.

In Figure 2.2, $K_0 \equiv$ initial capital stock; $K_{1,2} \equiv$ capital stock at end of periods 1,2; and $K^* \equiv$ long-run equilibrium capital stock. Starting off from an initial equilibrium position A with zero investment, a fall in the rate of interest shifts out the demand price schedule. Given an upward-sloping industry supply function, S_0, this causes the price of capital goods and investment to rise. At the end of the period the new

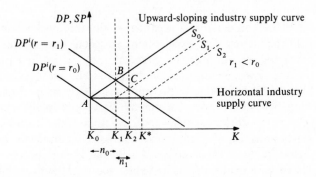

Figure 2.2

equilibrium position is B, with investment $n_0 = K_1 - K_0$ having taken place. At the beginning of period 2 there is initial capital stock K_1 which, together with given supply conditions (S_1), produces the new equilibrium position C. Investment $n_1 = K_2 - K_1$ is therefore carried out in period 2. This process continues until the long-run desired capital stock, K^*, is reached. For both a horizontal and upward-sloping industry supply curve the same long-run equilibrium is reached. However, with the horizontal supply curve adjustment is instantaneous with investment $K^* - K_0$ in the first period, while the response is spread out over time with the upward-sloping industry supply curve. Also, the initial investment $K_1 - K_0$ is less. Thus, the effect of a rising supply price of capital goods is to depress the interest elasticity of (actual) investment while investment demand remains as responsive as ever. We shall see in the following chapter that these basic insights carry over in a more sophisticated model intended to capture the distinctive elements of Keynes. As stated at the beginning, this must include a proper treatment of the role of expectations, and it is to this question that we now turn.

How do expectations enter into Keynes's investment theory, and how can his stress upon expectations be reconciled with the derivation above of a simple inverse relationship between the rate of interest and rate of investment? The answer to the first question is clear: expectations enter through the demand price term. Keynes emphasizes that the durability of capital equipment implies that uncertain future returns must be considered, and it is through this channel that the 'economic future is linked to the present'. Changed expectations of future returns will therefore change the demand price of capital assets and hence the equilibrium rate of investment at any given rate of interest. Plainly, in deriving a negative relationship between investment and the interest rate, expectations are being held constant.

Support for the adoption of this methodology lies in Keynes's idiosyncratic views on uncertainty and expectations (see Keynes 1936, Chs. 11 and 12; 1937). Broadly, two approaches have been adopted in modelling behaviour under uncertainty. First, one might suppose that, because the world is actually uncertain (individuals do not know what will happen), agents themselves are subjectively uncertain. In this approach individual's beliefs concerning the outcome of an action are represented by a probability distribution showing the probabilities attached to different random outcomes. Agents' behaviour can be modelled as if maximizing the expected value of some objective function (profits, utility, etc.), defined as the weighted sum of net benefits attached to different outcomes where the weights are the probabilities of those different outcomes occurring.

Alternatively, despite there being objective uncertainty, agents' behaviour may be represented as if they are subjectively certain and have point expectations about the future. It is this latter approach that is closest to Keynes. Distinguishing between risk and uncertainty, Keynes argued that in the face of uncertainty it may be not just wrong but actually impossible for entrepreneurs to calculate the probabilities required:

By uncertain knowledge . . . I do not mean merely to distinguish what is known for certain from what is only probable. The game of roulette is not subject, in this sense, to uncertainty, nor is the prospect of a Victory Bond being drawn. . . . The sense in which I am using the term is that in which the prospect of a European war is uncertain, or the price of copper and the rate of interest twenty years hence. . . . About these matters there is no scientific basis on which to form any capable probability whatever. We simply do not know. [Keynes 1937]

Such uncertainty is, however, inherent in the decisions of entrepreneurs; and the way individuals manage, argued Keynes, is to adopt rules of thumb that amount to taking some particular view of the future and, while recognizing its flimsy basis, acting upon it. It is the negation of the idea that entrepreneurs continually go through the process of calculating probabilities that is captured by the term 'animal spirits':

Most, probably, of our decisions to do something positive, the full consequences of which will be drawn out over many days to come, can only be taken as a result of animal spirits—of a spontaneous urge to action rather than inaction, and not as the outcome of a weighted average of quantitative benefits multiplied by quantitative probabilities. [Keynes 1936, 161]

Given this view of uncertainty, one cannot say why individuals' views of the future are what they are, or in what manner they will change, although one can recognize that new information may lead them to change their view of the future. This change in expectations may be substantial given the lack of a scientific basis upon which views of the future rest. The method Keynes adopted to deal with this problem was, in much of the *General Theory*, to treat expectations as exogenous (see also Begg 1982a, 1982b) and to solve the system for a given state of expectation. It is perhaps in his theory of investment that we get the clearest example of this, and it explains separate consideration of changes in the rate of interest for a given state of expectation, as above, and changes in expectations described as waves of optimism and pessimism on the part of the business community.

3 Witte

We now turn to a popular exposition of Keynesian investment theory, namely Witte (1963), and I shall argue that, as first pointed out by Marshall, Sampson, and Sedgwick (1975), it contains an inconsistency, typical of earlier theoretical work, in trying to force Keynesian investment theory into a comparative-statics framework. A consistent exposition of the Witte work requires a fully dynamic theory which is the subject of the next chapter.

The concern of the Witte paper is to establish 'the microfoundations of the social investment function'. That is, Witte wishes to establish an inverse relationship between investment and the rate of interest in a manner consistent with the theory of the firm. As he says, 'if there exists no microeconomic foundation for the aggregate investment function the economist who continues to employ the latter is implicitly rejecting the traditional theory of the firm as incorrect or at least as irrelevant.' The dilemma that Witte is trying to resolve is that the theory of the firm gives a demand for capital services and so implicitly a demand for capital stock. While a change in the rate of interest, say, will therefore imply a change in the desired capital stock, without further assumptions the theory of the firm is silent on the question of the rate at which the firm should move from one position to the other, namely, the rate of investment.

Following Keynes, Witte's insight is as follows. The firm's demand is for capital services and hence for capital stock. We can therefore derive a downward-sloping demand curve for capital for the individual firm from conventional theory. Aggregation of individual firm demand curves then gives the aggregate demand curve for capital stock. With the capital stock given in the very short run, equilibrium requires that the market price of capital goods be such that individual firms are willing to hold the entire stock of capital goods. Thus, the equilibrium price is given by the intersection of the aggregate demand curve for capital stock, DD, and the momentary stock supply schedule, SS, in Figure 2.3, where $d_i \equiv$ the stock demand curve for capital of the ith firm.

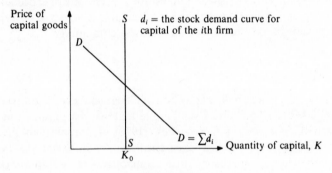

Figure 2.3

Equilibrium also requires that producers be on their supply curve and therefore that suppliers of capital goods adjust their output in response to the price determined on the demand side of the market. The rate of investment is then given by the rate of output of the capital-goods-supplying industry. The complete derivation of the investment schedule can be clearly seen in Figure 2.4. Witte concludes: 'the essential point is that the rate of investment decision, as opposed to the optimum stock decision, is made by the capital-goods-producing industry.'

The article is important for a number of reasons. First, Witte sees and stresses that the Keynesian investment function is a market equilibrium curve and hence is concerned with actual investment and

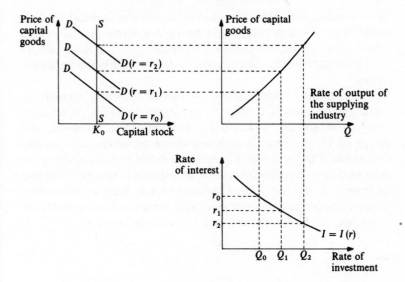

Figure 2.4

not investment demand. The representation shows clearly that, as in Keynes, equilibrium is characterized by the equality of demand and supply price. Second, he notes that the aggregate investment function cannot be obtained by simple addition of individual firm schedules: 'From this point of view the Keynesian investment function is derived by a quite unspecified process of aggregation from the micro-investment function. Such a view is questionable.' We have already seen the correctness of these insights.

Despite this, there a number of criticisms to be made. First, as Witte himself acknowledges, the model is concerned just with the short run, where increments to the capital stock brought about by positive net investment are negligible. Second, there is no explicit treatment of expectations. Since swings in expectation affect the demand price, a change in expectation could be represented only by a shift in the stock demand curve, *DD*. As we shall see in the next chapter, this fails to allow for the important distinction between anticipated and un-anticipated events. Third, and following on from this, there is a more fundamental criticism to be made, not only of Witte but of any representation of Keynesian investment theory that employs a comparative-statics framework. We can place in this category those who conclude with Haavelmo that no investment demand function exists since this argument, as Jorgenson has firmly pointed out, is based upon a comparative-statics argument. As such, these authors are concerned with the comparison of different equilibrium stationary states.

To see the inconsistency inherent in such an approach, it is useful to adopt the neoclassical framework of Jorgenson (1963), the assumptions of which are now familiar (see Marshall, Sampson, and Sedgwick 1975). Using this approach we can derive the static demand for capital, which is the capital stock that would be maintained by the firm were there no adjustment costs, in response to the prevailing rate of interest, r, and the price of capital goods, q. Since we are using a comparative-statics approach, no change is expected in q and r (or the wage rate, w). Hence, the first-order conditions become

$$F_L(\cdot) = \frac{\partial Q}{\partial L} = w \tag{8}$$

$$F_K(\cdot) = \frac{\partial Q}{\partial K} = q(r+\delta) = c \tag{9}$$

where the wage rate and price of capital goods are now measured taking the consumption good as numeraire.

In the dynamic framework adopted in the Jorgenson work, where the firm maximizes net worth, we get the more general first-order conditions for the firm that we saw in Chapter 1:

$$F_L(\cdot) = w \tag{10}$$

$$F_K(\cdot) = q(r+\delta) - \dot{q}^e. \tag{11}$$

Comparing the two sets of first-order conditions, we can see that the comparative-statics framework implies that entrepreneurs calculate the implicit rental of capital services, c, and hence adjust their capital stock, on the assumption that $\dot{q}^e = 0$. We can see therefore that this makes the comparative-statics framework inconsistent for analysing a Keynesian theory of investment; firms are calculating their optimal capital stock assuming that capital goods prices will not change ($\dot{q}^e = 0$), while, because of capacity constraints in the supplying industry, the theory implies that if the capital stock is changing then so too will the price of capital goods, and the final equilibrium price will, in general, be different from the initial price of capital goods.

This argument is quite general and does not rely upon the special assumptions of the neoclassical model. Thus, the Witte approach, and more generally the comparative-statics framework, is untenable, resting on an assumption which the model itself implies does not hold. We must therefore switch to a dynamic approach if we are consistently to derive the Keynesian investment schedule.

4 Conclusion

In this chapter I have set out Keynes's theory of investment in some detail. The distinctive elements of the theory are the consideration of how the behaviour of the capital-goods-producing industry influences aggregate investment and also the importance of entrepreneurial expectations. This latter point must be considered in the context of Keynes's particular views on behaviour under uncertainty. The modern trends in the modern investment literature, summarized in Chapter 1, have ignored this question of supply-side behaviour, and have concentrated instead on a careful specification of the variables that influence the demand for capital goods.

Despite this, typical expositions of Keynesian investment theory have correctly stressed the importance of supply-side considerations but have neglected the question of expectations. At its most basic, this is demonstrated in an inconsistency inherent in work that seeks to force Keynesian investment theory into a comparative-statics framework, since this means ignoring the changing price of capital goods which the theory predicts. More generally, the analysis makes no allowance for a distinction between anticipated and unanticipated changes, let alone being capable of capturing something of the idea of 'animal spirits'. In the next chapter we shall seek to remedy this by looking at a model that introduces supply-side behaviour in the form of an upward-sloping supply function for the capital-goods-producing industry and also assumes rational expectations. We shall see that this allows us to produce a consistent representation of Keynes and, in the neoclassical framework, a model of greater sophistication than the original Jorgenson contribution, because expectations become important.

Notes

1. For the relative merits of the internal rate of return and present value criteria, see Hirshleifer (1970).
2. I am grateful to Christopher J. Bliss for letting me see his lecture notes on this point.

3

The Implications of a Marriage of Jorgenson and Keynes

1 Introduction

The previous chapter examined a representative exposition of Keynesian investment theory in the light of the arguments presented by Keynes in the *General Theory*. I argued that the treatment of expectations was inadequate, capable of being dealt with at best by a simple shift in the demand curve for capital stock. In general, little attention has been paid to this aspect of Keynes's theory. We also saw that use of a comparative-statics framework to expound Keynes's investment theory is inconsistent, a view with which Jorgenson strongly concurs. Indeed, he doubts whether the Keynesian investment function can recover:

To complete the rehabilitation of the Keynesian marginal efficiency of investment schedule, interpreted as the level of investment resulting from a market equilibrium in investment goods corresponding to a given rate of interest, market equilibrium must be studied in a fully dynamic setting. The demand for investment goods must be derived from a comparison among alternative paths of optimal capital accumulation. It remains to be seen whether such a rehabilitation can be carried out in an internally consistent way. [Jorgenson 1966]

Jorgenson himself has, of course, put forward a theory which he argues consistently produces an investment function by using comparative-dynamic analysis but which, nevertheless, has received substantial criticism. The original version of his theoretical work assumed a putty–putty technology and no costs of adjustment, yielding the famous myopic property of his investment theory. Later Jorgenson (1972) argued that a more appropriate assumption would be that of adjustment costs, with the result that firm behaviour is no

---

The basis of this chapter was first presented in Precious (1979), which in turn draws upon Marshall, Sampson, and Sedgwick (1975).

longer myopic.[1] Firms must look forward, since, by smoothing any investment path, costs of adjustment can be reduced.

In this chapter I shall argue that a Keynesian theory of investment can be consistently presented in the perhaps unlikely surroundings of Jorgenson's neoclassical world without recourse to the assumption of strictly convex costs of adjustment, which finds no support in the *General Theory*. The solution of the model permits an interesting re-interpretation of Witte's original contribution which, for unanticipated events, removes the inconsistency that I argued was present in that work. Furthermore, it allows a proper consideration of the role of expectations which is crucial to Keynes, and the treatment of which is necessarily lacking in the original version of Jorgenson given the myopic behaviour on the part of firms. The model also therefore has more to offer than the original Jorgenson contribution. The work of this chapter looks at market equilibrium assuming given supply conditions; although I do not do so here, it is also possible to extend the work to a more general equilibrium setting and make allowance for investment on the part of the capital-goods-producing industry to influence supply conditions (see Mirrlees (1975), Precious (1985a)).

2 The Model

As in Jorgenson (1963), we shall assume: (1) a putty–putty technology with production function $Q(t) = F\{K(t), L(t); t\}$ which exhibits decreasing returns to scale; (2) that there are competitive conditions so that firms are price-takers in all markets including the capital market; (3) that there are no costs involved in either the sale or the purchase of investment goods or in the installation of new capital; and (4) that there are no taxes. Not all of these assumptions are necessary in what follows.

The firm is assumed to maximize net worth, $V(\cdot)$, subject to the constraints of the production function and the equation of motion for the capital stock.[2] Thus the firm's maximization problem,[3] taking the consumption good as numeraire, and therefore setting its price equal to unity, is:

$$\max V(t) = \int_t^\infty \{Q(s) - w(s)L(s) - q(s)I(s)\} \exp\left\{-\int_t^s r(u)du\right\} ds$$

subject to

$$(1)$$

$$Q(t) = F\{K(t), L(t), t\} \quad \forall t$$

and

$$\dot{K}(t) = I(t) - \delta K(t) \quad \forall t.$$

The first-order conditions are well-known:

$$F_K(t) = q(t)(r+\delta) - \dot{q}(t) \tag{2}$$

$$F_L(t) = w(t). \tag{3}$$

These first-order conditions are usually assumed to hold for an individual firm, but in competitive conditions we can treat a collection of price-taking firms as if they were a single price-taking unit (assuming no distortions in the production sector). Thus it is legitimate to treat the supplies and demands as coming from one vertically integrated firm. We do not, though, give any monopoly power to this single firm since it really stands for a collection of several small ones. The industry, or relevant sector, will therefore be in equilibrium if (2) and (3) hold with $F(\cdot)$ re-interpreted as aggregates.

Taking account of the *supply side* of the economy, there is now a second equilibrium relationship that must be satisfied. If we assume, following Keynes, that industry supply is a positive function of the price of capital goods and that, at the industry level, flow supply equals flow demand at all points of time, then we have

$$\dot{K}(t) = I\{q(t)\} - \delta K(t) \tag{4}$$

where $I\{q(t)\}$ is the industry supply function.

Expressions (2) and (4) must both be satisfied in order to give overall equilibrium. Since they are a pair of differential equations describing the movement of q and K through time, we can use these equations to draw a phase diagram describing the time paths of q and K along which both (2) and (4) are satisfied (see Figure 3.1).[4] The long-

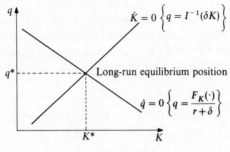

Figure 3.1

run equilibrium position is where both q and K are constant and hence at the intersection of the $\dot{q} = 0$ and $\dot{K} = 0$ loci in the figure. The $\dot{K} = 0$ locus is drawn upward-sloping since from (4) the combinations of q and K that imply $\dot{K} = 0$ are given by

$$I\{q(t)\} = \delta K(t). \tag{5}$$

Therefore the slope of the locus will depend upon δ, the depreciation rate, and the properties of the supply function. As in Keynes, we assume that $\partial I(\cdot)/\partial q > 0$, and since $\delta > 0$, q and K must both increase to satisfy (5). Hence the $\dot{K} = 0$ is upward-sloping.

Similarly, the $\dot{q} = 0$ locus is drawn downward-sloping since, along the $\dot{q} = 0$ locus,

$$q = \frac{F_K}{r + \delta} \tag{6}$$

and so $dq/dK < 0$ for a decreasing-returns-to-scale production function.

It remains to show how q and K move at any point in the diagram. We do this as follows. First, consider the behaviour of K. At any point above the $\dot{K} = 0$ locus, such as point A in Figure 3.2(a), the price of capital goods is greater than that which gives $\dot{K} = 0$. In other words, since $I'(q) > 0$ and $\dot{K} = I(q) - \delta K$, the price of capital goods induces a supply of investment goods greater than amount δK and hence the capital stock is growing: $\dot{K} > 0$. Similarly, at any point below the $\dot{K} = 0$ locus, such as point B in Figure 3.2 (a), the price of capital goods calls forth investment less than that which gives $\dot{K} = 0$, and hence the capital stock is shrinking: $\dot{K} < 0$. The arrows of motion are therefore as drawn in the diagram.

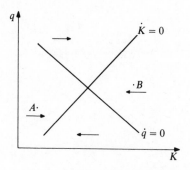

Figure 3.2(a)

Next, consider the movement of q. Since $\dot{q} = q(r + \delta) - F_K(\cdot)$, then at any point above the $\dot{q} = 0$ locus, such as A' in Figure 3.2(a), we can see that the price of capital goods is greater than that which gives $\dot{q} = 0$. Therefore $q(r + \delta) > F_K(\cdot)$ and hence $\dot{q} > 0$. In other words, since the marginal product of capital is less than the interest and depreciation cost of using capital, firms must be expecting capital gains in order to be willing to hold the existing capital stock. Thus q is rising at all points above and similarly falling at all points below the $\dot{q} = 0$ locus as indicated in the diagram.

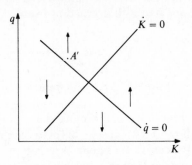

Figure 3.2(b)

We now simply draw these conclusions together and, combining Figures 2(a) and 2(b), can determine how (q, K) *move at any point in the phase diagram.* Along any of the paths drawn in Figure 3.3, both equilibrium conditions are satisfied so that both demanders and

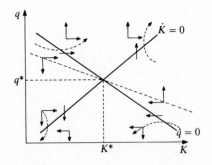

Figure 3.3

suppliers of capital goods are on their (notional) demand and supply curves. However, we can see that the model has what is called a 'saddlepoint' solution, which means that there is only one stable path that leads to the steady state and in that sense the model has a unique equilibrium. On all other paths either the price of capital goods or the capital stock becomes infinite or zero. Long-run stability therefore requires that demanding and supplying firms are not myopic but look into the future and so ensure that the economy moves along the stable path.[5]

We are now in a position to examine the effects of a change in the rate of interest upon the level of investment.

(a) An Unexpected Change in the Rate of Interest

Suppose, initially, that we are in long-run equilibrium at point A in Figure 3.4 and let the rate of interest unexpectedly fall from r_0 to r_1, where managers expect the new rate of interest to persist. The lower interest rate increases the present value of returns to any unit of capital and so shifts the $\dot{q} = 0$ locus up, giving a new long-run equilibrium position at C. In order to move to the new steady state along the unique rational expectations path, where anticipations are subsequently realized, the system must move instantaneously to point B on the new stable path. This is the *only continuous path leading to steady state*. Hence the price of capital goods jumps immediately to q' and falls thereafter at a diminishing rate. At B, although $F_K > q(r + \delta)$, firms remain in equilibrium because of capital losses. We can therefore draw in the time path of capital goods prices (Figure 3.5).

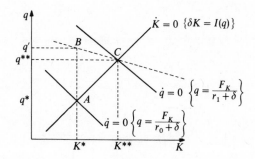

Figure 3.4

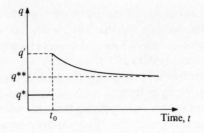

Figure 3.5

From the equilibrium condition that suppliers of investment goods are on their notional supply curves, we can, knowing the path of q, plot the time path of investment (Figure 3.6).

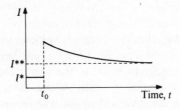

Figure 3.6

The growth in capital stock depends upon the difference between gross investment $I\{q(t)\}$ and replacement investment, $\delta K(t)$. Since along the stable path q is falling and K rising, the rate of increase in K becomes smaller and smaller, which explains the time path drawn for K (Figure 3.7).

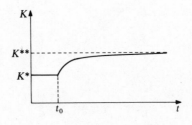

Figure 3.7

It is apparent from the analysis that, the greater the fall in the rate of interest, the larger the total capital stock adjustment and the greater the rate of investment at each point in time. In other words, we can determine the rate of investment not just at the instant of change in the rate of interest, t_0, but also at each moment thereafter. But this means that, as requested by Jorgenson at the outset, we have an investment function 'derived from a comparison among alternative paths of capital accumulation'.

In summary, a Keynesian marginal efficiency of investment schedule, defined by Jorgenson as 'the level of investment resulting from a market equilibrium in investment goods', has been consistently derived using a comparative-dynamic framework.

(b) A Reconsideration of the Witte Analysis

It is appropriate at this stage to return to the Witte analysis. Witte ignores the effect of net investment upon the capital stock of demanding firms and so considers only the instantaneous effects of different rates of interest upon the rate of investment. As we saw, the result is that, the larger the fall in the rate of interest, the higher the new equilibrium price of capital goods and hence the higher the rate of investment, all of which is contained in the above analysis. Extending the Witte analysis to allow for the effects of investment upon the capital stock would give the same qualitative results as above. A growing capital stock would, for the new given demand curve for capital stock, lead to falling capital goods prices and hence a falling rate of investment. This process would continue until a new equilibrium was reached where the price of capital goods had fallen sufficiently to just induce a flow supply of new investment goods equal to the required replacement investment.

The fault with the Witte analysis was the inconsistency of analysing a Keynesian theory of investment in a comparative-statics framework. Given the model of this chapter, in using a comparative-statics framework one is implicitly using the first-order condition

$$F_K = q(r + \delta).$$

In other words, one is assuming that $\dot{q} = 0$ whereas, as the phase diagram makes plain and a Keynesian model implies, if $\dot{K} \neq 0$ then

$\dot{q} \neq 0$. The appropriate equilibrium condition is

$$F_K = q(r+\delta) - \dot{q}$$

and, given the earlier analysis, we see that in this case one simply cannot define, independently of supply conditions, a price at which rational investors are willing to hold the existing capital stock. One cannot, as with usual demand and supply functions, draw the demand curve for capital independently of supply.

Witte's implicit assumption that $\dot{q} = 0$ implies that his demand curve for capital stock (drawn in Figure 2.4 above) is given by the $\dot{q} = 0$ locus in the phase diagram. For Witte, a fall in the rate of interest shifts up the demand curve, and the new equilibrium price of capital goods is given from the $\dot{q} = 0$ locus. In fact, we have seen that a consistent analysis implies that the $\dot{q} = 0$ locus does indeed shift up but that the new equilibrium price, which leaves firms on their demand curve for capital stock, is given by the stable path rather than the $\dot{q} = 0$ locus. Furthermore, for this case of a once-and-for-all unanticipated change in the rate of interest (or other relevant exogenous variables), we can *re-interpret the demand curve drawn by Witte as the stable path of the phase diagram.* Having done this, one can proceed entirely consistently exactly as Witte does; that is, given the initial capital stock, we can read off the equilibrium price of capital goods and hence the rate of investment from the upward-sloping industry supply function.[6] We shall see shortly that this conclusion does not carry over for the case of anticipated changes in exogenous variables.

In the previous chapter we reached the conclusion, in a simplified presentation, that, if there is a rising supply curve for new capital goods, the interest elasticity of actual investment will be reduced. Following on from this, the phase diagram can also be used to show that this conclusion holds in the market model above. Consistent analysis of the behaviour of investment requires, because of the upward-sloping industry supply function, that recognition be given to the changing price of capital goods. However, normal analysis of the competitive firm that faces a perfectly elastic supply curve implies that $\dot{q} = 0$. Thus, taking account of the $\dot{q}$ term takes us from the $\dot{q} = 0$ locus to the stable path in the phase diagram, from which, comparing the two paths, it can be seen that, in response to a change in the rate of interest, the movement in the price of capital goods and hence investment is depressed.

We shall now move on to consider the role of expectations in the market model.

(c) An Expected Change in the Rate of Interest

Consider now an anticipated change in the rate of interest where, at time t_0, firms get news of a fall in the rate of interest which will occur at time t_1. For the special case of a constant rate of interest, r_0, (2) can be rewritten:

$$q(t) = \int_t^\infty F_K(s) \exp\{-(r_0 + \delta)(s - t)\} \, ds. \tag{7}$$

This simply shows that in equilibrium firms are indifferent between renting and buying capital assets. The generalization of (7) to allow for a variable rate of interest is

$$q(t) = \int_t^\infty F_K(s) \exp\left\{-\delta(s - t) - \int_t^s r(\tau) \, d\tau\right\} ds \tag{8}$$

and for the particular case considered here of a fall in the rate of interest from r_0 to r_1, expected to occur at t_1, we can write (8) as

$$q(t) = \int_t^{t_1} F_K(s) \exp\{-(r_0 + \delta)(s - t)\} \, ds$$

$$+ \exp\{-(r_0 + \delta)(t_1 - t)\} \int_{t_1}^\infty F_K(s)$$

$$\times \exp\{-(r_1 + \delta)(s - t)\} \, ds. \tag{9}$$

Differentiating (9) with respect to t gives[7]

$$\dot{q}(t) = q(t)(r_0 + \delta) - F_K(t). \tag{10}$$

(10) holds for all $t < t_1$. Once the change in the rate of interest occurs, we have

$$q(t) = \int_t^\infty F_K(s) \exp\{-(r_1 + \delta)(s - t)\} \, ds \quad \forall t \geq t_1 \tag{11}$$

and therefore, differentiating with respect to t,

$$\dot{q}(t) = q(t)(r_1 + \delta) - F_K(t) \quad \forall t \geq t_1. \tag{12}$$

Summarizing the above, we can say that for all $t < t_1$ the firm is driven by equation of motion (10), which therefore remains exactly as before the change in expectation. For $t \geqslant t_1$ the behaviour of the firm is governed by the equation of motion (12). The diagram for this case is shown in Figure 3.8, where

$$r_1 < r_0$$

$$r = r_0 \quad \forall t < t_1$$

$$r = r_1 \quad \forall t \geqslant t_1.$$

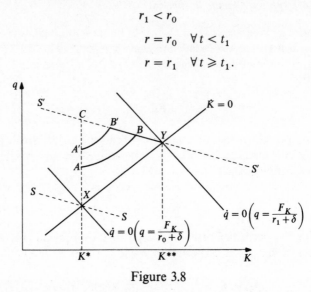

Figure 3.8

Since for all $t \geqslant t_1$ the equation of motion (12) becomes relevant, firms must, at t_1, be on the new stable path $S'S'$. Exactly as before, this becomes the new unique path to long-run equilibrium.

To understand the behaviour of the system for $t < t_1$, it is instructive to consider time paths for q and K that cannot be followed. One obvious path satisfying the equations of motion at all points of time would be for the system to remain at rest at S until time t_1, when q would jump to point C and continue down the new stable path $S'S'$ thereafter. Alternatively, had the system been initially out of long-run equilibrium but on the stable path SS, then behaviour consistent with equations of motion (10) and (12) would have been to continue down SS for all $t < t_1$ with q jumping to the new stable path $S'S'$ at t_1.

Both of these paths can be ruled out because they imply a discontinuous path. On a discontinuous path, either the jump to the stable path is unanticipated at the initial date, in which case we cannot describe the path as compatible with perfect foresight, or it is anticipated. If it is anticipated, this implies foreseen capital gains to be made at time t_1. Firms would therefore have an incentive to purchase capital goods an instant earlier, forcing the price to rise then. This argument can, of course, be repeated all the way back to time t_0, and it tells us that there can be no anticipated discrete jumps in q. Reaction to news in the form of discrete jumps in q is instantaneous. Thereafter, in the absence of new information, q must follow a continuous path.

The following sequence of events illustrated in Figure 3.8 must therefore occur in response to the anticipated fall in the rate of interest. Suppose the system is initially in long-run equilibrium at X. In response to the news at t_0 of a change in the rate of interest at t_1, there is an immediate jump in q. Then, for $t_0 \leqslant t < t_1$, the movement of (q, K) is governed by the equations of motion (4) and (10). Finally, since we know that at t_1 the system must be on the new stable path $S'S'$, the jump in q must be such that (q, K) governed by (4), (10) just hit the new stable path at t_1. In this way, anticipated jumps in q are avoided. In Figure 3.8 AB is one such path; $A'B'$ is another, drawn when the interval between t_0 and t_1 is smaller since it takes less time to move along $A'B'$ than AB, reflecting the higher investment and therefore faster growth in capital stock along such a path. In the limit, the gap between t_0 and t_1 is zero and so the change in the rate of interest is unanticipated. The system therefore jumps immediately to C on the new stable path as before. The jump in q gets larger as the interval of time between the news of the event and the actual fall in the rate of interest gets smaller, simply reflecting the higher present value of machines, more of whose returns are discounted by a lower rate of interest.

(d) A Comparison with Jorgenson

We now compare the predictions of the market model and Jorgenson for the case of an unexpected change in the rate of interest which is expected to persist. Jorgenson analyses such a case using the comparative-dynamic framework as in this chapter. In his most complete statement of the neoclassical theory, he argues:

We assume that all changes of the rate of interest are precisely compensated by changes in the rate of change of the price of current and future investment goods so as to leave the own-rate-of-interest on investment goods unchanged. Under this condition the discounted value of all future capital services which is equal to the current price of investment goods is left unchanged by variations in the time path of the rate of interest. The condition that the time path of the own-rate-of-interest on investment goods is left unchanged by a change in the time path of the rate of interest implies that forward prices or discounted future prices of both investment goods and capital services are left unchanged by variations in the rate of interest. [Jorgenson 1966]

I have already outlined the argument in Chapter 1. Briefly, as we saw there, if the unexpected change in the rate of interest occurs at t_0, the Jorgensonian adjustment process is that $\dot{q}(t_0)$ accommodates the change in r, leaving the cost of capital

$$c(t_0) = q(t_0)\left\{r + \delta - \frac{\dot{q}(t_0)}{q(t_0)}\right\}$$

unchanged. With $q(t_0)$, $c(t_0)$ constant this implies, from the definition of $c(\cdot)$, that future capital goods prices will be lower. And, because $(r + \delta - (\dot{q}/q))$ is, by assumption, unchanged by variations in the rate of interest for all future t, this implies that any future c will also be lower than otherwise. To maintain the equilibrium condition $F_K(t) = c(t)$, firms will therefore desire higher capital stocks, implying a higher rate of investment. By comparison of such alternative paths for the capital stock, we can conclude that investment is inversely related to the rate of interest.

An immediate objection to Jorgenson is the seemingly arbitrary nature of such an adjustment process since, as Tobin (1966) objects, 'There is no reason to assume that expected prices of goods accommodate themselves so obligingly to interest rate variations.' In fact, the assumption is rather implausible. The lower rate of interest, which causes capital stocks and investment to be higher than otherwise, leads to lower new capital goods prices at all future dates.

By contrast, the model presented in this chapter, which similarly derives an investment function by comparative dynamics, does have an adjustment mechanism for which there is a good theoretical basis. Furthermore, the structure of the model is firmly neoclassical, being supplemented only by another standard competitive assumption— namely, an upward-sloping industry supply function. In this model *both* $q(t_0)$ and $\dot{q}(t_0)$ change in response to an unexpected change in the rate of interest at time t_0. The price of capital goods is immediately forced up by increased demand, reflecting higher discounted profits, and declines thereafter as supply is increased and hence marginal products fall.

The contrast between Jorgenson and the market model is highlighted when we consider responses to an anticipated change in the rate of interest. While he appears not to explicitly address this question, the earlier statement that 'We assume that *all* changes in the rate of interest are precisely compensated . . .' (italics added) would appear to be quite general. Applied to the case of an expected change in the rate of interest, this assumption has the effect of insulating the present from the future. The price of capital goods is simply the discounted value of all future capital rentals, which on this assumption is left unchanged.

Also, since the rate of change of the price of investment goods varies with the rate of interest, it implies that capital rentals are left unchanged until the instant after the rate of interest actually changes. Investment therefore responds to an anticipated change only when that change actually occurs and, as in Witte, the difference between expected and unexpected changes is irrelevant.

An implication of all this is that the 'myopic' property of Jorgenson's neoclassical world has to be carefully considered. It is usual, as we saw in Chapter 1, to argue that Jorgenson's firms exhibit myopic behaviour because the assumption of a putty–putty technology leads to the well-known first-order conditions which depends only upon current variables, so that future events do not influence the current behaviour of firms. We have now seen in this chapter why I claimed earlier that it is not the assumption of putty–putty *per se* that implies myopic behaviour. The market model, which assumes a putty–putty technology, has exactly the same myopic first-order conditions, and yet firms respond immediately to anticipated events. Even though individual firms have no market power, prices adjust immediately to news of any changes with current capital goods prices and their rate of change *summarizing information about expected returns* over the life of the machine. It is only because Jorgenson makes the additional assumption about the behaviour of capital goods prices that firms are also myopic in the sense of not reacting to anticipated events.

(e) A Comparison with Keynes

We now consider the legitimacy of describing the market model as a representation of Keynes's investment theory. In this respect it has several noteworthy features. Most obviously, an upward-sloping industry supply function for new capital goods is included in the analysis and leads to appropriately 'Keynesian' results. Thus, there is a gradual response on the part of firms to both expected and unexpected changes in the economic environment, and the interest elasticity of investment is appropriately reduced. The analysis also has the important merit of being consistent, in that it has demanding firms taking full account of the changing price of capital goods implied by the model.

The most obvious drawback of the model as a representation of Keynes is the assumption of the neoclassical framework, which has been amply criticized and would be seen by many as un-Keynesian. A defence can nevertheless be made of this procedure. There are three aspects of the neoclassical model that are distinctive. The first, often claimed as a merit of the approach, is the assumption of perfectly competitive optimizing firms. This carries with it the implication that firms are unconstrained and so seems to be at odds with those who view Keynes as believing in generalized market non-clearing with, therefore, the possibility of excess supply in the goods market and firms being demand-constrained. In fact, the model used by Keynes in the *General Theory* admits market non-clearing in the labour market but assumes that prices are sufficiently flexible to ensure goods market clearance (see also Bliss 1975). This is made explicit by Keynes at the outset in his adherence to Classical Postulate I and his equilibrium condition for investment, since both imply goods market equilibrium. We can also advance the absence from the *General Theory* of any notion of the accelerator theory of investment requiring, as it does, some form of demand constraint as evidence of Keynes's belief in a basically competitive framework. It is a more recent extension of the ideas of Keynes to consider generalized market non-clearing, which so far has been confined to a mainly static analysis as in Malinvaud (1977). In the remaining chapters of this book I shall similarly broaden the analysis and go on to consider rigorously the investment decisions of firms that face rationing in the goods and labour markets.

Second, and most important, I have analysed the investment decisions of firms in a rational expectations (perfect foresight) framework despite Keynes's emphasis upon uncertainty and expectations in entrepreneurs' decisions. The previous chapter outlined Keynes's argument that individuals were unable to form reasonable probability judgements about uncertain events, and hence that their actions are best described by the term 'animal spirits' rather than expected utility maximization. This means that we cannot predict what agents' expectations will be or how they will be revised in response to new information, although we can recognize that this revision may be quite abrupt, given their weak basis. Because of this, Keynes often found it convenient to treat expectations as given and to work out the solution of the model on this assumption.

In this chapter we have seen that rational expectations models are capable of giving proper consideration to the question of expectations, showing the full dynamic response of firms to both anticipated and unanticipated events. While the spirit of rational expectations is un-Keynesian, the view that important aspects of this assumption are nevertheless compatible with the *General Theory* has been persuasively argued by Begg:

Any unique rational expectations path is conditional on a given information set at the date expectations are to be formed, and it is only in response to exogenous 'news'. In this sense, if one collapses the notion of a given path, along which changes are entirely anticipated, to the notion of a given state of expectation, then a rational expectations equilibrium is one in which current endogenous variables depend upon a given set of expectations about the future, and comparative dynamics proceeds by imagining an exogenous change in expectations . . . The second aspect of the rational expectations assumption with which the *General Theory* is compatible is the insistence that changes in expectation, in the above sense, are necessarily unpredictable given current information. It is impossible to construct a theory of how information will be revised. [Begg 1982b]

Finally, the presence of a unique rational expectations path means that it is simultaneously impossible to predict how agents will revise their expectations while, nevertheless, being able to determine individuals' expectations currently given the information set. This last feature, in contrast to the indeterminancy of expectations in the *General Theory*, is clearly advantageous for modelling purposes.

Third, Jorgenson assumes a putty–putty technology. Given the assumptions of perfect markets and no adjustment costs, this either implies instantaneous adjustment and therefore an infinite rate of investment or, making Jorgenson's price adjustment assumption, means that anticipated changes do not influence current behaviour. While a putty–clay technology may indeed be more appropriate, it is not the assumption of putty–putty *per se* that gives the above conclusions. I have shown how a determinate rate of investment can be derived and, in a rational expectations framework, how expected events will influence current behaviour.

3 Conclusion

In this chapter we have considered an investment model that amends the early work of Jorgenson by the additional assumption of an upward-sloping industry supply function as suggested in Keynes. This neoclassical framework proves capable of providing a consistent Keynesian investment theory, contrary to the doubts expressed by Jorgenson quoted at the beginning of the chapter. As a representation of Keynes, the model gives an important role to expectations and is capable of taking seriously the notion of animal spirits which summarizes Keynes theory of entrepreneurial behaviour under uncertainty found in the *General Theory*. Distinguishing between anticipated and unanticipated changes allows a re-interpretation of earlier work by Witte, which it is shown can be seen as a consistent analysis of the special case of permanent unanticipated exogenous changes.

The model also compares favourably with the original Jorgenson theory by allowing expectations of future events an important influence upon current investment and shows that Jorgenson's 'myopic' first-order condition is quite consistent with non-myopic behaviour. Finally, although I have not done so here, it is possible to extend the model and make it symmetric by allowing for changes in the capacity of the capital goods industry (see Precious 1985; Mirrlees 1975). Although this adds some complexity, the qualitative results are unaltered and it shows how the rational expectations techniques of this chapter can be used in two-sector growth models.

Appendix A   The Intertemporal Optimization Problem for the Unconstrained Neoclassical Firm

The firm is trying to maximize its objective function (net revenue) through time while subject to the constraints of (i) its technology, which describes the production possibilities Q from a given quantity of capital, K, and labour, L, and (ii) the equation of motion of the capital stock describing how the capital stock changes as investment occurs, given that there is a constant rate of depreciation of capital, δ. Most students will be familiar with the use of Lagrangean techniques to solve static optimization problems and will be relieved to hear that essentially the same method generalizes to this intertemporal optimization problem.

In the static optimization problem, such as

$$\max \pi = PQ - wL$$

subject to

$$Q = F(\bar{K}, L)$$

where $\bar{K}$ = fixed capital stock, we form the Lagrangean by introducing new variables—Lagrange multipliers, one for each constraint—and find a saddlepoint for this expression. Thus

$$\mathscr{L} = pQ - wL + \lambda\{Q - F(\bar{K}, L)\}$$

$$\therefore \frac{\partial \mathscr{L}}{\partial Q} = 0 \Rightarrow p + \lambda = 0$$

$$\frac{\partial \mathscr{L}}{\partial L} = 0 \Rightarrow -w - \lambda F_L(\cdot) = 0$$

or $$w/p = F_L(\cdot).$$

Which is the usual static equilibrium condition that the real wage equal the marginal production of labour.

The method we use here, forming a *Hamiltonian function*, is an extension of the method of Lagrange multipliers to dynamic optimization problems.

The problem,

$$\max V(t) = \int_t^\infty \{p(t)Q(t) - w(t)L(t) - q(t)I(t)\}e^{-rt}\,dt$$

subject to

$$Q(t) = F\{K(t), L(t)\}$$

and

$$\dot{K}(t) = I(t) - \delta K(t),$$

is, as can be seen, the intertemporal extension of the simple static profit maximization problem we solved above. The firm must maximize net worth through time subject to constraints that hold at each point of time. To solve this, we form the Hamiltonian function as follows:

$$H = pQ - wL - qI + \lambda\{Q - F(K, L)\} + \mu(I - \delta K).$$

We deal with the constraint of the technology exactly as before. Note, however, that we deal with the constraint expressing the equation of motion of the capital stock (ii) slightly differently. The first-order conditions for this problem are, as before,

$$
\begin{cases}
\dfrac{\partial H}{\partial Q} = 0 \Rightarrow p + \lambda = 0 \\[2mm]
\dfrac{\partial H}{\partial L} = 0 \Rightarrow -w - \lambda F_L(\cdot) = 0.
\end{cases}
$$

Now we have a new choice variable, I, and therefore, analogously,

$$
\frac{\partial H}{\partial I} = 0 \Rightarrow -q + \mu = 0.
$$

Finally, we have an additional FOC:

$$
\frac{d(\mu e^{-rt})}{dt} = \frac{-\partial H\, e^{-rt}}{\partial K}
$$

which implies

$$
\dot{\mu} e^{-rt} - r\mu e^{-rt} = -(-\lambda_1 F_K - \delta\mu) e^{-rt}
$$

$$
\therefore \quad \dot{\mu} = \mu(r + \delta) + \lambda_1 F_K.
$$

Solutions of these equations gives

$$
\dot{q} = q(r + \delta) - p\, F_K(\cdot)
$$

and

$$
\frac{w}{p} = F_L(\cdot).
$$

as in the text.

This basic structure for the solution of the firm's intertemporal optimization problem will be repeated, with one small variation (to be explained later), in each chapter.

Appendix B   An Intuitive Explanation of the Step from Equation (9) to Equation (10)

In Chapter 1. (pp. 9–11 and Note 1, pp. 21, 22) we saw that the discrete-time equivalent of the first-order condition

$$
\dot{q}(t) = q(r + \delta) - F_K(\cdot)
$$

was

$$
q(t) = \frac{p(t+1)\, F_K(t+1)}{1+r} + q(t+1)\left(\frac{1-\delta}{1+r}\right)
$$

and of

$$q(t) = \int_t^\infty p(s) F_K(s) \exp\{-(r+\delta)(s-t)\}\, ds$$

it was

$$q(t) = \sum_{i=0}^\infty \frac{p(t+i) F_K(t+i)}{1+r} \left(\frac{1-\delta}{1+r}\right)^i.$$

In this chapter we are considering the case of a variable interest rate, and the generalization of the above constant interest rate expressions contained in equations (8), (9), and (10) is again easily seen in terms of its discrete-time equivalent.

For a constant interest rate r_0, we already know that

$$q(t) = \frac{p(t+1) F_K(t+1)}{1+r_0} + q(t+1)\left(\frac{1-\delta}{1+r_0}\right) \qquad \text{(i)}$$

which implies

$$q(t) = \sum_{i=0}^\infty \frac{p(t+i) F_K(t+i)}{(1+r_0)} \left(\frac{1-\delta}{1+r_0}\right). \qquad \text{(ii)}$$

Suppose, to keep things simple, and without loss of generality, the anticipated change in the interest rate (from r_0 to r_1) is expected to occur in period $t+2$. Then (ii) becomes

$$q(t) = \frac{p(t+1) F_K(t+1)}{1+r_0} + \frac{p(t+2) F_K(t+2)}{1+r_0}\left(\frac{1-\delta}{1+r_1}\right) + \ldots \text{(etc.).}$$

$$\text{(iii)}$$

But

$$q(t+1) = \frac{p(t+2) F_K(t+2)}{1+r_1} + \frac{p(t+3) F_K(t+3)}{1+r_1}\left(\frac{1-\delta}{1+r_1}\right) + \ldots$$

$$\text{(iii}')$$

Subtracting (iii$'$) from (iii) gives

$$q(t) = \frac{p(t+1) F_K(t+1)}{1+r_0} + q(t+1)\left(\frac{1-\delta}{1+r_0}\right). \qquad \text{(iv)}$$

Which is exactly the same as (i) despite the anticipated interest rate change. In words, the equation of motion for $q(\cdot)$ at time t is *unaffected by the anticipation of an interest rate change*, which is what (10) says (in continuous time). Equations (8), (9), etc. and subsequent derivations may therefore look complicated but in reality are not.

Notes

1. I shall deal extensively with the adjustment cost version of the model in Chapters 5–8.
2. I assume rational expectations, which in this deterministic framework is equivalent to the assumption of perfect foresight.
3. This is the first time I have formally presented the optimization problem of the Jorgenson firm, and it is worth spending some time in deriving the results since the same basic technique can readily be grasped and is used in each of the remaining chapters. See Appendix A at the end of this chapter.
4. This is the first time I have made use of phase diagrams and therefore I explain them in some detail. The technique is used extensively in later chapters. See also Begg (1982a) for a good discussion of the role of phase diagrams in rational expectations models.
5. This saddlepoint property is a standard feature of rational expectations models. See Begg (1982a Ch. 3) for further discussion. I return to this question of the unique rational expectations path in Chapter 8.
6. I'm grateful to John Fleming for this point.
7. This rather complicated-looking derivation is nothing more than an extension of the reasoning of Chapter 1 (pp. 9–11 and pp. 21, 22). See Appendix B at the end of this chapter.

4

Keynes, '*q*' Theory, and Market Non-clearing: The Relationship between Investment and Stock Market Value

1 Introduction

The literature on investment over the last two decades has been dominated by the neoclassical theory originating with Jorgenson and, more recently, by the '*q*' theory of Tobin, which I mentioned briefly in Chapter 1. We shall now look at Tobin's work in more detail.

'*q*' is the ratio of the post-tax real rate of return on capital to its cost and is consequently a measure of the incentive to acquire new capital. The higher the rate of return on new capital goods relative to their cost, the greater the profit to be made and hence the higher the rate of investment will be. Tobin argued that:

Economic logic indicates that a normal equilibrium value for *q* is 1 for reproducible assets. Values of *q* above 1 should stimulate investment in excess of requirements for replacement and normal growth and values of *q* below 1 should discourage investment. [Tobin and Brainard 1977, 238]

In its best-known form, '*q*' has been measured by the ratio of the stock market value of the firm to the replacement cost of its capital stock, and it is therefore argued that there is a positive link between the stock market value of the firm and investment. Such a view is echoed in Chapter 12 of the *General Theory*:

The daily revaluations of the Stock Exchange, though they are primarily made to facilitate transfers of old investments between one individual and another, inevitably exert a decisive influence on the rate of current investment. For there is no sense in building up a new enterprise at a cost greater than that at which a similar enterprise can be purchased; whilst there is an inducement to spend on a new project what may seem an extravagant, sum, if it can be floated off on the Stock Exchange at an immediate profit. [Keynes 1936, 151]

For Tobin, '*q*' is a crucial variable which links the real and financial sectors of the economy. Monetary policy, for instance, works in the Tobin framework by reducing interest rates, raising stock market values relative to the cost of new physical equipment, and hence increasing 'q' and stimulating investment.

Let us now, however, be more precise and call the ratio of the stock market value of the firm to the replacement cost of its capital stock, *average* 'q'. Average 'q' is therefore a measure of the firm's existing capital stock and may not be a good guide to investment, which is determined by the profitability of acquiring *new* physical assets. It was realized by Tobin therefore that the concept relevant for investment is *marginal* 'q', defined as the ratio of the market value of new additional investment goods to their replacement cost (Tobin and Brainard 1977, 243). While marginal and average 'q' will often move together, this will not always be the case, as I shall prove rigorously later in the chapter. One important practical example occurred in the early 1970s with the large and unexpected increase in oil prices. Firms that had invested in equipment that involved high energy consumption saw their stock market values fall considerably. Nevertheless, the incentive, for both these firms and others, to invest in energy-saving capital was high.

Appropriately reformulated in terms of marginal 'q', it is clear that, for the rate of investment to be an increasing function of 'q', some sort of adjustment costs must be assumed. If a firm can freely change its capital stock, then it will do so until 'q' is equal to unity in the absence of taxation.

In fact, we can show a remarkable link between some of the theories of investment we have looked at so far: although Tobin's 'q' theory was not originally rigorously derived from the firm's optimization problem, Abel (1979) showed that *the neoclassical investment theory modified by the assumption of adjustment costs and the 'q' theory are equivalent.*[1] The argument is straightforward. Taking capital goods as the numeraire, and therefore setting their price equal to unity, marginal 'q' (at time t) in a neoclassical world is just equal to[2]

$$q(t) = \int_t^\infty \frac{\partial \pi(s)}{\partial K(s)} \exp\left\{-(r+\delta)(s-t)\right\} ds \qquad (1)$$

where $\partial \pi(s)/\partial K(s) \equiv$ the marginal return from a unit of capital at time s. Hence, with the price of capital goods set at unity, (1) is the ratio of the discounted marginal returns from a unit of capital to the replacement cost, i.e. marginal 'q'. But the firm will go on investing until the marginal benefit from doing so is equal to the marginal cost. If we assume that the adjustment costs associated with investment at rate $I(t)$ are $C\{I(t)\}$, this will be when

$$1 + C'\{I(t)\} = \int_t^\infty \frac{\partial \pi(s)}{\partial K(s)} \exp\{-(r+\delta)(s-t)\} ds \qquad (2)$$

and therefore, since $C''(\cdot) > 0$, $I = I(q)$ where $\partial I/\partial q > 0$. Hence the neoclassical theory augmented by adjustment costs implies a determinate rate of investment which is an increasing function of 'q'.

We have seen in the previous chapter that it is also possible to provide a determinate rate of investment in the neoclassical model without recourse to the assumption of strictly convex costs of adjustment. The mechanism is a changing price of capital goods as the capital-goods-producing industry moves along an upward-sloping supply function. The attraction of this *Keynesian* amendment to Jorgenson's original theory[3] is that it provides a more plausible account of price adjustment, focusing as it does on price determination in a rational expectations framework. We also saw that anticipations of the future can play an important role, and hence that the unrealistic myopic property of Jorgenson's original formulation disappears. As a representation of Keynes, we saw that such a market model provided an internally consistent theory by taking seriously this question of movemnts in the price of capital goods. The absence of the concept of adjustment costs from the *General Theory* leads Tobin to recognize that 'q' theory is 'a different investment theory from what appears to be the Keynesian investment function of the *General Theory*', although his immediately subsequent argument, that 'Keynes' condition that the marginal efficiency of capital equal the rate of interest determines not the flow of investment but the stock of capital' (Tobin and Brainard 1977, 244), ignores the insight of Witte that we can read off the level of investment from the industry supply function.

One way of representing the difference between the cost of adjustment story (generalized neoclassical) and the market model is in terms of the behaviour of the capital goods market. Both the upward-sloping industry supply function and costs of adjustment lead firms to smooth their investments and imply that expectations are important. In the market model it is assumed that the capital goods market clears continuously with suppliers on their notional supply curves for capital goods. The price of capital goods is determined endogenously and, given the industry supply function, determines investment. By contrast, by relating investment to 'q', which tells of the incentive to invest on the part of demanding firms, we are looking at the demand function for investment. In this story investment is demand-determined and hence there is an implicit assumption of 'sticky' capital goods prices with the possibility of producers being off their notional supply curves.[4]

This question of the implicit assumption being made about market conditions is an important one, particularly in the context of the investment equations used in empirical work. Broadly, summarizing the results of the earlier chapters, we can say that differences over three main sets of assumptions—about the technology, market conditions, and the nature of expectations formation—divided previous formulations of the investment equation. For those theories using an optimizing framework, derivation of the first-order conditions gives a present-value condition relating the marginal costs and benefits of investing. Different assumptions lead to different first-order conditions, and hence manipulation of the present-value criterion yields the appropriate variables for the investment equation used in empirical work. Perhaps the best example of this is in Jorgenson with the assumption of a putty–putty technology. This leads to the present-value condition[5]

$$p^I(r+\delta) = p\frac{\partial F}{\partial K}(\cdot) + \dot{p}^I,$$

manipulation of which leads to one formulation of the investment equation. The putty–clay assumption yields a different first-order condition and investment equation. Similarly, different assumptions about market conditions—for instance, about whether the firm is modelled as cost-minimizing and hence demand-constrained or as profit-maximizing and unconstrained—lead to different functional forms for the present-value condition and hence investment equation. Included under this heading are accelerator theories which, although often not derived in an optimizing framework (but see Grossman 1972), require some form of demand constraint and so lead to a different form of investment equation than that for the unconstrained firm. Finally, different expectations formation assumptions clearly lead to different investment equations. For instance, the assumption of adaptive expectations, as well as of delivery lags, was used to justify the introduction of lagged variables which an assumption of static or rational expectations would have precluded.

On a theoretical level, Tobin's '*q*' theory, defined in terms of *marginal* '*q*', is quite general and not only can be consistent with the neoclassical theory extended to include the assumption of adjustment costs, but also can be with (for example) the putty–clay model. The insight of Abel can be generalized: equation (2) says that adjustment costs introduce a wedge between demand and supply price and implies that investment will be an increasing function of the ratio of demand to supply price, that is, '*q*'. In equation (2) I have made a specific assumption about the firm's technology (putty–putty) which implies that the demand price term is defined by

$$\int_t^\infty \frac{\partial \pi(s)}{\partial K(s)} \exp\left\{-(r+\delta)(s-t)\right\} ds.$$

However, by changing the assumption about the firm's technology from putty–putty to putty–clay, we simply change the expression for the demand price without affecting the logic of the argument.

The real attraction of '*q*' theory was that the original formulation of '*q*' in terms of stock market value relative to replacement cost of capital (i.e. average '*q*') seemed to offer a solution to the problem surrounding the empirical testing of investment theories. Suddenly, it looked as if asset markets could be relied upon to digest all relevant expectations and reflect them in stock market prices. Empirical work could therefore use an *observable market variable to summarize all the information concerning expectations formation, market conditions, and technology* which had divided previous formulations of the investment equation. There have now been a considerable number of empirical studies based on some variant of Tobin's '*q*': see for instance Jenkinson (1981), Oulton (1981), Ciccolo (1975), and von Furstenberg (1977). This popularity has not been matched, however, by equal attention to the question of precisely which expectations are being summarized by Tobin's '*q*' and hence as to what is being implicitly assumed in this empirical work.

In fact, the early optimism that, by using the average '*q*' formulation of Tobin's theory, one could use market data to capture all relevant information, and so avoid the disputes about the appropriate assumptions to be used, is now known to be unfounded. Hayashi (1982) has given a rigorous analysis of the relationship between average and marginal '*q*' and has established conditions under which marginal '*q*' can be inferred from market data. He showed that it was appropriate to proxy marginal by average '*q*' under conditions of a *putty–putty technology, constant returns to scale, and perfect competition*. In other words, unless these strong assumptions hold, marginal and average '*q*' are not equal, and hence investment will not be related to the stock market value of the firm in the manner suggested by traditional 'q' theory. More recently, Edwards and Keen (1983) have shown that even this specification ignores personal taxation and assumes that investment is financed entirely by retentions. They show that, when account is taken of differential taxation, marginal 'q', like the cost of capital, depends sensitively upon the marginal source of finance. Thus the problems that this causes for the specification of investment equations in terms of the cost of capital also arise when implementing a 'q'-based investment theory. These problems, they conclude, have not always been fully appreciated by those using 'q'.

In the same way, researchers who have regressed investment against average 'q' in the hope of being able to bypass specification problems about market conditions have neglected the fact that similar problems arise in the specification of 'q'. In the following section I shall therefore clarify the relationship between marginal and average 'q' under different market conditions for a neoclassical firm. By allowing for the possibility of disequilibrium in goods and labour markets, we generalize Hayashi's result to include market non-clearing. It is shown that the relationship between marginal and average 'q', and therefore the appropriate form of the investment equation, depends upon market conditions, both current and anticipated. If markets do not clear continuously, marginal and average 'q' are not equal, with the divergence reflecting the extent of rationing; and hence investment cannot be straightforwardly related to the stock market value of the firm. In the remaining chapters I shall pursue this theme of market non-clearance and extend 'q' theory by presenting a unified analysis of the investment behaviour of a firm faced with the possibility of rationing in the output, labour, and capital goods market.

2   Optimal Capital Accumulation in the Presence of Rationing and a Generalized Hayashi Result

Consider, as in the previous chapter, a neoclassical firm acting to maximize the present value of cash flows, V, where in order to focus on the implications of rationing we ignore taxation:

$$V(t) = \int_t^\infty \{p(s)Q(s) - w(s)L(s) - p^I(s)I(s)\} \exp\left\{-\int_t^s r(u)du\right\}ds$$

$$(3)$$

where p, w, and p^I are the prices of output, labour, and investment goods, respectively; Q, L, and I are output, labour, and investment; and r is the interest rate.

The firm is assumed to have a constant-returns-to-scale production function:

$$Q(t) = F\{K(t), L(t); t\} \qquad (4)$$

and, following Hayashi, we introduce adjustment costs[6] by assuming

$$\dot{K}(t) = \psi\{I(t), K(t), t\} - \delta K(t). \qquad (5)$$

In other words, I units of gross investment do not necessarily turn into capital: only $\psi \times 100$ per cent of investment does.

The firm takes as given the sequence of wages, prices, and real interest rates $(w, p, p_I, r)_{t = 0, \ldots, \infty}$. In order to introduce rationing we assume, as in Barro and Grossman (1971), Malinvaud (1977), and Blanchard and Sachs (1982), that firms not only take as given both current and anticipated prices but also take as given the quantity constraints that they may face. Firms may face constraints either in the output market on the quantity of goods they can sell, in the labour market on the labour it can hire or fire, or in the capital goods market on the rate of investment that firms can undertake. The sequence of possible constraints can be written $(\bar{Q}, \bar{L}, \bar{I})_{t = 0, \ldots, \infty}$.

The firm's optimization problem is therefore, as in Chapter 3, to maximize (3) subject to the constraint of the technology (4) and the equation of motion for the capital stock (5); and we now add the potential quantity constraints it faces:[7, 8]

$$\max_{Q, I, L} V(0) = \int_0^\infty \{p(t)Q(t) - w(t)L(t) - p^I(t)I(t)\} \exp\left\{ - \int_0^t r(s)ds \right\} dt \qquad (6)$$

subject to

$$\dot{K}(t) = \psi(I, K; t) - \delta K(t) \, \forall t$$

$$Q(t) \leqslant \bar{Q}(t); L(t) \leqslant \bar{L}(t); I(t) \leqslant \bar{I}(t) \, \forall t$$

and

$$Q(t) = F(K, L; t) \, \forall t.$$

Following Arrow and Kurz (1970), we can write the Hamiltonian, H, as

$$H = pF(K, L) - wL - p^I I + \mu\{\psi(I, K) - \delta K\} \qquad (7)$$

and the Lagrangean, $\mathcal{L}$, as

$$\mathcal{L} = H + \lambda_1\{\bar{Q} - F(K, L)\} + \lambda_2(\bar{L} - L) + \lambda_3(\bar{I} - I). \qquad (8)$$

The first-order conditions for this problem are

K:
$$\frac{d(\mu e^{-rt})}{dt} = \frac{-\partial \mathscr{L} e^{-rt}}{\partial K}$$

$$\Rightarrow \dot{\mu} = \mu\{r + \delta - \psi_K(\cdot)\} - (p - \lambda_1) F_K(\cdot). \tag{9}$$

L:
$$\frac{\partial \mathscr{L}}{\partial L} = 0 \Rightarrow (p - \lambda_1) F_L(\cdot) = w + \lambda_2. \tag{10}$$

I:
$$\frac{\partial \mathscr{L}}{\partial I} = 0 \Rightarrow p^I + \lambda_3 = \mu \psi_I(\cdot). \tag{11}$$

$$\left.\begin{array}{l} \bar{Q} \geqslant Q, \lambda_1 \geqslant 0 \\[4pt] \bar{L} \geqslant L; \lambda_2 \geqslant 0 \\[4pt] \bar{I} \geqslant I; \lambda_3 \geqslant 0 \end{array}\right\} \quad \text{with complementary slackness.} \tag{12}$$

Equation (9) says that μ is the present discounted value of additional future profits resulting from an additional unit of capital. The extra profits result not just from extra productive capacity represented by the term $(p - \lambda_1) F_K(\cdot)$ but also from installation cost savings represented by the $\psi_K(\cdot)$ term. This can be seen most clearly by rewriting (9) as[9]

$$\mu(t) = \int_t^\infty \{p(s) - \lambda_1(s)\} F_K(s) \exp[-\{r + \delta - \psi_K(s)\}(s - t)] \, ds. \tag{9'}$$

λ_1 reflects the fact that the firm may be demand-constrained, which creates a wedge between $\mu(t)$ and the discounted marginal revenue products the firm would earn if free to sell output, i.e.

$$\int_t^\infty p(s) F_K(s) \exp[-\{r + \delta - \psi_K(s)\}(s - t)] \, ds.$$

Equation (10) is the marginal productivity of labour condition and says that, in the absence of any constraints, the firm equates the real wage and the marginal product of labour. However, in the presence of a constraint in either the output market on the quantity of goods to be sold or the labour market, the marginal product of labour will be greater than the real wage with the extent of the divergence depending on the severity of rationing in standard fashion.

As in Hayashi, we can rewrite (11) to read

$$p^I + \{1 - \psi_I(\cdot)\}\mu = \mu - \lambda_3 \tag{11'}$$

which simply says that, in the absence of rationing from the investment goods market ($\lambda_3 = 0$), the marginal benefit from investment should equal the marginal cost of that investment. It can be seen that the marginal cost consists of two terms: first, the straightforward purchase price of the machine, p^I; second, the adjustment costs associated with the investment. If there are no adjustment costs, $\psi_I(\cdot)$ = 1 and the market value of the firm would increase by μ for one additional unit of investment. But in fact, the capital stock increased by only $\psi_I(\cdot)$. Thus $(1 - \psi_I)\mu$ represents the market value forgone owing to adjustment costs. The term λ_3 in (11) again represents the effect of rationing and says that, if constrained over the rate of investment, then (by definition) the marginal costs and benefits of investment are not equal.

It is now straightforward to derive a generalization of the Hayashi result, which is as follows:[10]

$$
\text{Marginal 'q' = average 'q'} - \frac{\displaystyle\int_t^\infty \lambda_1(s)Q(s)\exp\{-r(s-t)\}\,ds}{p^I(t)K(t)}
$$

$$
- \frac{\displaystyle\int_t^\infty \lambda_2(s)L(s)\exp\{-r(s-t)\}\,ds}{p^I(t)K(t)}
$$

$$
- \frac{\displaystyle\int_t^\infty \lambda_3(s)I(s)\exp\{-r(s-t)\}\,ds}{p^I(t)K(t)} \tag{13}
$$

where marginal 'q' at time $t = \mu(t)/p^I(t)$ and average 'q' at t is Tobin's 'q' as defined above, namely, $V(t)/p^I(t)K(t)$.

3   Conclusion

There are several things to be said about this result. First, it is a straightforward generalization of Hayashi and shows that marginal and average 'q' differ if firms are rationed. Indeed, in the subsequent chapters I shall present plausible circumstances in which they move in opposite directions. Second, and following on from this, it has been made clear that in empirical analysis work using 'q' theory does not evade the problems faced in earlier studies on investment. Old questions as to whether, say, the firm is demand-constrained or not, and therefore whether the investment function should be derived by cost minimization or profit maximization, must still be answered. The host of investment equations containing exogenous demand terms with the implicit assumption of a sales constraint stands in contrast to the more recent spate of investment equations using average 'q' with therefore the implicit assumption of no demand (or any other) constraint. The problem of the appropriate assumption to use is well recognized in the usual specification of investment equations. In the recent rush to implement 'q'-based investment theories it has perhaps not been fully appreciated that this alternative approach encounters the same problems.

Appendix A The Intertemporal Optimization Problem for the Constrained Neoclassical Firm

The maximization problem expressed here is simply the intertemporal optimization of Chapter 3 (see Appendix A) extended to take account of inequality constraints. As before, it is helpful to consider the static optimization problem first. The static equivalent of this problem is (taking account *only* of a possible sales constraint, that is, ignoring possible rationing in the labour and capital goods markets, for simplicity):

$$\max \pi = pQ - wL \qquad \text{(i)}$$

subject to $Q = F(\bar{K}, L)$ and $Q \leqslant \bar{Q}$,

which says that the firm is looking to maximize profits subject to the constraint of the technology and the sales constraint that the firm must always produce less than or no more than the amount demanded. The problem is therefore one of maximization subject to an inequality constraint, and this is solved by introducing a new Lagrangean multiplier to take account of the additional (potential) constraint, and by forming the Lagrangean

$$\mathscr{L} = pQ - wL + \lambda_1 \{Q - F(\bar{K}, L)\} + \lambda_2 (\bar{Q} - Q). \qquad \text{(ii)}$$

The first-order conditions become

$$\frac{\partial \mathscr{L}}{\partial Q} = 0 \Rightarrow p + \lambda_1 - \lambda_2 = 0 \qquad \text{(iii)}$$

$$\frac{\partial \mathscr{L}}{\partial L} = 0 \Rightarrow -w - \lambda_1 F_L(\cdot) = 0 \qquad \text{(iv)}$$

and, finally, and extra condition:

$$\lambda_2(\bar{Q} - Q) = 0; \quad \lambda_2 \geqslant 0. \tag{v}$$

Solving these, we have

$$\frac{w}{p - \lambda_2} = F_L(\cdot) \quad \text{and} \quad \lambda_2(\bar{Q} - Q) = 0.$$

What do these first-order conditions expressing the optimal policy of a static firm facing a possible sales constraint say? First, when $\lambda_2 = 0$, that is, when $\bar{Q} > Q$ and therefore the firm is unconstrained, $w/p = F_L(\cdot)$ exactly as before. However, when desired output is greater than the level of demand, then actual output will be equal to $\bar{Q}$ and the firm will be constrained, which is expressed, from (v), by λ_2 being positive. But $\lambda_2 > 0$ implies from (iii), (iv) that $w < pF_L(\cdot)$. In other words, because of the output constraint, the firm has been unable to go on expanding output until the marginal cost of labour equals the marginal benefit. The firm would like to expand output and take on more labour, but is constrained from doing so since it cannot sell any more output.

The intertemporal extension of this is exactly analogous. We amend the Hamiltonian of Appendix A in Chapter 3 to take account of the quantity constraints that may now hold at each point of time, by introducing a new variable (multiplier) as in equation (8), and the first-order conditions are as shown.

Appendix B   A Proof of the Generalized Hayashi Result in Equation (13)

Differentiating (3) with respect to time gives (ignoring timescripts)

$$\dot{V} - rV = -(pQ - wL - p^I I). \tag{i}$$

Since $F(K, L)$ is a constant-returns-to-scale production function, $F(\cdot) = F_K K + F_L L$ and so

$$\dot{V} - rV = -\{p(F_K K + F_L L) - wL - p^I I\}. \tag{ii}$$

Substituting for $F_K(\cdot)$, $F_L(\cdot)$ from (9), (10) and rearranging gives

$$-(\dot{V} - rV)(p - \lambda_1) = pK\mu(r + \delta) - pK\dot{\mu} + p(w + \lambda_2)L$$
$$- (p - \lambda_1)wL - p^I I(p - \lambda_1). \tag{iii}$$

Substituting for $p^I I$ from (11) and cancelling terms in wpL,

$$-(\dot{V} - rV)(p - \lambda_1) = pK\mu(r + \delta) - pK\dot{\mu} + p\lambda_2 L$$
$$+ p\lambda_3 I + \lambda_1(wL + p^I I)$$
$$- p\mu\{\psi_I(\cdot)I + \psi_K(\cdot)K\}. \qquad \text{(iv)}$$

Assumption of a constant-returns-to-scale adjustment cost function implies that

$$\psi_I I + \psi_K K = \dot{K} + \delta K. \qquad \text{(v)}$$

Substituting in, cancelling terms in $pK\mu\delta$, and taking $\lambda_1(\dot{V} - rV)$ over to the right-hand side gives

$$-(\dot{V} - rV)p = pK\mu r - pK\dot{\mu} - p\mu\dot{K} + p(\lambda_2 L + \lambda_3 I)$$
$$+ \lambda_1(wL + p^I I) - \lambda_1(\dot{V} - rV). \qquad \text{(vi)}$$

Dividing through by p, and noting from (i) that $wL + p^I I = \dot{V} - rV + pQ$, we get

$$\dot{V} - rV = -(K\mu r - K\dot{\mu} - \mu\dot{K}) - \lambda_1 Q - \lambda_2 L - \lambda_3 I. \qquad \text{(vii)}$$

Therefore

$$(V - \dot{\mu}K) = r(V - \mu K) - (\lambda_1 Q + \lambda_2 L + \lambda_3 I) \qquad \text{(viii)}$$

which can be rewritten (again using the trick of Ch. 1, n. 1)

$$V(t) - \mu(t)K(t) = \int_t^\infty \{\lambda_1(s)Q(s) + \lambda_2(s)L(s)$$
$$+ \lambda_3(s)I(s)\} \exp\{-r(s - t)\}\,ds.$$

Hence,

$$\frac{\mu(t)}{p^I(t)} = \frac{V(t)}{p^I(t)K(t)} - \frac{\displaystyle\int_t^\infty \lambda_1(s)Q(s)\exp\{-r(s - t)\}\,ds}{p^I(t)K(t)}$$

$$- \frac{\displaystyle\int_t^\infty \lambda_2(s)L(s)\exp\{-r(s - t)\}\,ds}{p(t)K(t)}$$

$$- \frac{\displaystyle\int_t^\infty \lambda_3(s)I(s)\exp\{-r(s - t)\}\,ds}{p^I(t)K(t)}. \qquad \text{(x)}$$

QED

Notes

1. As was hinted in Ch. 1.
2. Assuming a constant interest rate.
3. As noted in the previous chapter, Jorgenson has subsequently argued the additional assumption of adjustment costs is appropriate for his theory: see Jorgenson (1972).
4. Of course, the two approaches can be combined. For more on this see Chapter 8.
5. To avoid notational confusion, I shall denote the price of capital goods as p^I.
6. Adjustment costs are more usually introduced by assuming, as in Lucas (1967), Gould (1968), and Treadway (1969), an adjustment cost function $C(I,K,t)$ which says that the cost of doing investment at rate I is $C(I,K)$ units of capital (where $C_I, C_{II} > 0$ and $C_K < 0$). The capital accumulation equation is now written

$$\dot{K} = I - \delta K$$

and the Hamiltonian becomes

$$H = \{pF(K,L) - wL - p^I C(I,K)\} + \mu(I - \delta K).$$

It is straightforward to show that the result of Section 2 still holds with this specification of adjustment costs.

7. The quantity constraints have been written in (6) as maximum constraints on Q, L, and I. It is equally possible to reverse the inequality sign in (6): see Chapter 7 on investment constraints.
8. See Appendix A at the end of this chapter for an intuitive explanation of the optimization problem.
9. We have already used this trick: see Chapter 1, n.1 and Chapter 3, Appendix B.
10. See Appendix B at the end of this chapter.

5

Demand and Employment Constraints, Rational Expectations, and Investment Theory

1 Introduction

We have now completed a thorough tour of previous theories of investment. In Chapter 3 we extended the Jorgenson model to produce a 'Keynesian' theory of investment capable of recognizing the importance of expectations and including the role of the capital-goods-producing industry. In Chapter 4 we looked at the relationship between the neoclassical, adjustment cost, and 'q' theories of investment and the implications for the relationship between the stock market value of the firm and the rate of investment.

In this chapter we shall continue a theme begun in Chapter 4 and tackle the problem of the lack of a general framework which allows one to analyse firms' investment decisions when markets may not clear. To date, investment theory has focused on two polar cases, characterized here as the cost minimization and profit maximization approaches. The former assumes that the firm minimizes the cost of meeting a given level of demand (see, e.g., Brechling 1975, Hausman 1973, Abel 1979) and has the attraction of enjoying the support that empirical work invariably finds for a sales or demand term in the investment equation (see, e.g., Bischoff 1971a, 1971b, Hausman 1973, Bean 1981). By contrast, the profit maximization approach makes the assumption that the firm faces no constraints on the quantity of goods that can be sold. (See, e.g., Brechling 1975, Jorgenson 1963, Abel 1979 for perfectly competitive models; Nickell 1978 looks at models where the firm has some market power in the product market.)

The purpose of this chapter is to present a *unified analysis* of these polar cases in a model where firms are neither always demand-constrained nor always unconstrained. There is therefore an important role for demand to play, as in the cost-minimizing models; but, like Malinvaud (1977), we are concerned primarily with those cases where the firm may switch regimes. The focus of attention is ultimately the firm's investment decision, but *en route* we shall also look at the behaviour of output and employment. This chapter therefore also provides a *general dynamic analysis of the firm which may be rationed in the goods market*.

To illustrate the generality of the analysis, I shall apply the same technique to consider the question of the investment behaviour of the firm that may be rationed in the labour market. Finally, in Chapter 7 and 8 below we shall consider the effect of constraints on the supply side of the capital goods market.

More generally, in terms of methodology, the diagrammatic presentation is an illustration of the use of phase diagrams to combine two, until recently, divergent strands of economic theory: namely, rational expectations and disequilibrium theory. As we shall see, it represents an extension of the work of Wilson (1979) and others in analysing anticipated changes within rational expectations models by phase diagrams.

The model that is presented builds on Abel (1979) and is extended by the inclusion of possible sales and employment constraints as in Blanchard and Sachs (1982). It is therefore a '*q*' theory model of investment extended to take account of disequilibrium in the product and labour markets. As such, the analysis represents the initial extension of the work of the previous chapter on the relationship between marginal and average '*q*' for a firm that faces rationing. The analysis of the firm should also be seen as complementary to the work of Neary and Stiglitz (1983), Malinvaud (1977, 1982) and Blanchard and Sachs (1982). Neary and Stiglitz extend Malinvaud (1977) to consider a two-period model which can include rationing in the goods and labour markets. They thus incorporate expectations into fix-price theory but cannot treat properly the investment decisions of firms, the importance of which is emphasized in Malinvaud (1982). Lastly, in an impressive paper, Blanchard and Sachs present a fully intertemporal general equilibrium model with slow adjustment of prices and thus rationing. However, their full model is beyond analytical tractability and can be solved only by numerical simulations. By taking the partial equilibrium approach adopted here, it is possible to make use of phase diagrams to analyse the investment, output, and employment decisions of the firm and give a detailed consideration to the dynamics of their response to disequilibrium.

The plan of the chapter is as follows. In Section 2 the firm's optimization problem is presented for a firm that faces rationing in the product market only, and the response of an always-unconstrained and always-constrained firm is reviewed. The behaviour of investment in these cases has been analysed by Abel (1979). My focus is different, since for the rest of the analysis attention must be paid to the output supply decision. Section 3 then outlines a unified analysis of the above two extremes and looks at the behaviour of a firm that will be switching between different regimes. In this chapter and the next we shall focus on two kinds of changes that have been given prominence elsewhere (Malinvaud 1977): changes in the level of demand, and changes in wage rates. We shall also look at the effects of interest rate variations. Section 4 moves on to the case of employment constraints, and Section 5 presents concluding remarks.

2 The Model

The firm is assumed to face given prices and levels of demand. Sometimes the level of demand will allow the firm to sell all it wishes at the given price, in which case the firm is unconstrained, and sometimes it will not, in which case the firm is demand-constrained. For the time being only a constraint on sales is considered, although the analysis is also applicable to labour market and capital goods market constraints, as we shall see in Section 4 and Chapters 7 and 8, respectively. In spite of the fact that the firm faces quantity constraints, there is assumed to be no reaction of prices to these constraints. This is of course a strong assumption, and some consideration will be given to dealing with price flexibility in Chapter 8. For now, the assumption is defended on the grounds, first, that it allows a diagrammatic presentation, since phase diagrams can be used, and, second, that it is interesting to consider the effects of demand constraints alone. How prices may then move and what effects this has is a further interesting problem. Finally, it is the implicit assumption already being made in cost minimization models.

Consider then a profit-maximizing firm with costly adjustment of capital and a putty–putty technology acting to maximize the present value of cash flows:

$$V(0) = \int_0^\infty \langle p(t)Q(t) - w(t)L(t) - [I(t) + C\{I(t)\}] \rangle e^{-rt} dt \quad (1)$$

where $Q(t)$, $L(t)$, and $I(t)$ are the output, employment, and investment respectively of the firm at time t, and $p(t)$, $w(t)$ are the price of output and wage rate, respectively. The price of capital goods is assumed to be unity. $C(I)$ are the adjustment costs associated with doing investment at rate I where the adjustment cost function $C(\cdot)$ is assumed to be strictly convex; and r is the firm's discount rate, here assumed constant for simplicity. To focus attention, we also ignore taxation.

The firm's maximization problem is:[1]

$$\max (1)$$

subject to
$$Q(t) = F\{K(t), L(t); t\} \tag{2a}$$

$$Q(t) \leqslant \bar{Q}(t) \tag{2b}$$

$$\dot{K}(t) = I(t) - \delta K(t) \tag{2c}$$

The three constraints reflect the constraint of the technology (2a), the assumption that the firm cannot sell more than the given level of demand $\bar{Q}$ (2b), and the equation of motion for the capital stock (2c), where $K(t)$ is the capital stock of the firm at time t and δ is the constant exponential rate of depreciation. Following Arrow and Kurz (1970), and as we have already seen in Chapter 4 this problem can be solved by forming the Lagrangean:

$$\mathscr{L} = [pF(K, L) - wL - \{I + C(I)\}] + \mu(I - \delta K) + \lambda\{\bar{Q} - F(K, L)\} \tag{3}$$

where we have substituted for $Q(\cdot)$ from (2a) and associated multipliers μ, λ with the constraints (2c) and (2b), respectively.

The first-order conditions for this problem are:

$$\frac{d(\mu e^{-rt})}{dt} = \frac{-\partial \mathscr{L} e^{-rt}}{\partial K} \Rightarrow \dot{\mu} = \mu(r + \delta) - (p - \lambda)F_K(\cdot) \tag{4}$$

$$\frac{\partial \mathscr{L}}{\partial L} = 0: \quad (p - \lambda)F_L(\cdot) = w \tag{5}$$

$$\frac{\partial \mathscr{L}}{\partial I} = 0: \quad \mu = 1 + C'(I) \tag{6}$$

$$\bar{Q} \geqslant Q: \quad \lambda \geqslant 0 \text{ with complementary slackness.} \tag{7}$$

Expression (4) can be rewritten as

$$\mu(t) = \int_t^\infty \{p(s) - \lambda(s)\} F_K(s) \exp\{-r(s - t)\} \, ds \tag{8}$$

and says that μ is the present discounted value of additional profits that are due to an additional unit of investment. Since the price of capital goods is assumed to be unity, μ *here represents marginal 'q' defined as the ratio of the market value of additional investment goods to their replacement cost.* Since $C''(\cdot) > 0$, (6) says that, *in this neoclassical model with adjustment costs, investment is an increasing function of marginal 'q'* as first shown formally by Abel (1979). We can therefore write $I = I(\mu)$ where $I'(\cdot) > 0$.

Equation (5) says that, if the firm is sales-constrained ($\lambda > 0$), it would like to expand output and take on labour and hence the marginal revenue product of labour is greater than the wage rate. Equation (7) simply says that sales cannot exceed the level of demand, and when desired output does so λ becomes positive, reflecting the firm being constrained.

There are therefore two separate cases to consider. First, when the firm is unconstrained ($Q < \bar{Q}$, $\lambda = 0$), then the first-order conditions can be summarized as

$$\dot{\mu} = \mu(r + \delta) - pF_K(\cdot); \; pF_L(\cdot) = w \tag{9a}$$

and

$$\dot{K} = I(\mu) - \delta K \tag{9b}$$

where we have simply substituted $I = I(\mu)$ from (6) into the equation of motion for the capital stock.

Second, for the constrained firm ($Q = \bar{Q}$, $\lambda > 0$), the first-order conditions become

$$\dot{\mu} = \mu(r + \delta) - (p - \lambda)F_K(\cdot); \; (p - \lambda)F_L(\cdot) = w \tag{10a}$$

$$\dot{K} = I(\mu) - \delta K. \tag{10b}$$

Substituting for $(p - \lambda)$ from the marginal productivity of labour condition, the equation of motion for μ becomes

$$\dot{\mu} = \mu(r + \delta) - \frac{wF_K(\cdot)}{F_L(\cdot)}. \tag{11}$$

(a) Investment, Output, and Employment of an Unconstrained Firm

Assume a constant-returns-to-scale Cobb–Douglas production function:

$$Q = K^\alpha L^{1-\alpha} \quad 0 < \alpha < 1$$

and so

$$F_L(\cdot) = (1-\alpha)\left(\frac{K}{L}\right)^\alpha; \; F_K(\cdot) = \alpha\left(\frac{K}{L}\right)^{\alpha-1}$$

Thus, from the marginal productivity of labour condition in (9a),

$$\frac{w}{p} = (1-\alpha)\left(\frac{K}{L}\right)^\alpha \tag{12}$$

and substituting for K/L from (12) into the equation of motion for μ gives

$$\dot{\mu} = \mu(r+\delta) - p\alpha\left(\frac{1}{1-\alpha}\frac{w}{p}\right)^{(\alpha-1)/\alpha} \tag{13}$$

(13) and (9b) are thus a pair of equations of motion for marginal 'q' (μ) and K which summarize the first-order conditions for an unconstrained firm and can be used to construct a phase diagram.

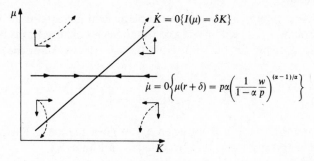

Figure 5.1

In Figure 5.1, the $\dot{K} = 0$ locus is drawn upward-sloping since along that locus $I(\mu) = \delta K$ and $\delta, I'(\cdot) > 0$. Along the $\dot{\mu} = 0$ locus

$$\mu(r+\delta) = p\alpha\left(\frac{1}{1-\alpha}\frac{w}{p}\right)^{(\alpha-1)/\alpha}$$

and thus the $\dot{\mu} = 0$ locus is horizontal, being independent of K. The motion of μ, K in the diagram can be determined as follows: at any point above the $\dot{\mu} = 0$ locus μ is rising, since

$$\mu(r+\delta) > p\alpha\left(\frac{1}{1-\alpha}\frac{w}{p}\right)^{(\alpha-1)/\alpha}$$

and therefore $\dot\mu > 0$; at any point above the $\dot K = 0$ locus K is increasing, since $I(\mu) > \delta K$ and so $\dot K > 0$. The system has a saddlepoint solution because, for any point above or below the $\dot\mu = 0$ locus, the system will blow up asymptotically and the only (stable) path to the long-run equilibrium or steady-state position A lies along the $\dot\mu = 0$ locus.

We, now use the phase diagram to investigate the response of the unconstrained firm to changes in prices. Abel (1979) has analysed the response of investment to changes in fiscal parameters in such a model, and for purposes of comparison we will be interested in the response of investment, but our main concern in this section will be the output decision of the firm. This will tell us what output firms would have liked to have undertaken in the absence of a sales constraint.

(b) The Response of the Unconstrained Firm to an Increase in the Wage Rate

Assume at time t_0 an unanticipated permanent increase in the wage rate from w_0 to w_1 with p and r constant. Such a change leaves the $\dot K = 0$ locus unaffected but shifts down the $\dot\mu = 0$ locus. Along the $\dot\mu = 0$ locus

$$\mu(r + \delta) = p\alpha\left(\frac{1}{1-\alpha}\frac{w}{p}\right)^{(\alpha-1)/\alpha}$$

and so an increase in w for given p, r, δ must reduce μ. The phase diagram therefore can be represented as in Figure 5.2.

Initially the firm is doing replacement investment just sufficient to maintain its steady-state capital stock, K^*. Following the increase in

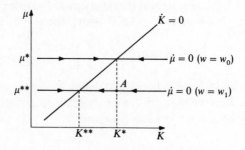

Figure 5.2

the wage to w_1, the rate of investment and μ fall instantaneously to a new constant lower level (point A in Fig. 5.2), causing the firm's capital stock to gradually decline to the new steady-state level K^{**}. The time paths of investment and the capital stock are shown in Figure 5.3.

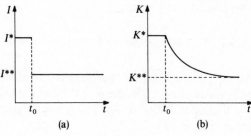

Figure 5.3

It is straightforward to see what is happening to the firm's output and employment at the same time. From the marginal productivity of labour condition (12), we know that the capital–labour ratio is determined by the real wage:

$$\frac{K}{L} = \left(\frac{1}{1-\alpha} \frac{w}{p} \right)^{\frac{1}{\alpha}}.$$

Thus when the wage rises, the capital–labour ratio must rise instantaneously to its new level, after which it remains constant. Since adjustment costs rule out infinite investment the capital stock is given instantaneously, and so the firm must shed labour and hence output must drop. Thereafter, from the phase diagram K gradually falls, and so, to keep K/L constant as required, L and therefore Q must be falling at the same rate. In response to an unanticipated permanent

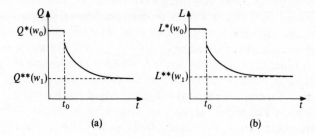

Figure 5.4

increase in the wage rate, therefore, output and employment of the unconstrained firm have the time paths shown in Figure 5.4.

For an unanticipated permanent increase in the wage rate, there is an instantaneous increase in the capital–labour ratio as employment and hence output is reduced. Thereafter Q, K, and L gradually fall to their new lower steady-state levels.

(c) The Response of the Unconstrained Firm to an Increase in the Rate of Interest

Consider at time t_0 an unanticipated permanent increase in the rate of interest with p, w constant. Again the $\dot{K} = 0$ locus is unaffected, and again the $\dot{\mu} = 0$ locus is shifted down. The phase diagram therefore looks as before (Figure 5.5).

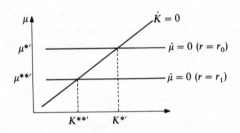

Figure 5.5

The response of μ, I, and K is qualitatively exactly the same as for the increase in the wage, and therefore it is not drawn. The response of the firm's employment and output is only slightly different. From the marginal productivity condition (12), the K/L ratio must remain unchanged since neither w nor p has changed. Since K does not change instantaneously, the firm in this case does not instantaneously alter its employment and output. After t_0, however, L and Q must, as before, follow a similar time path to that of K, which is known from the phase diagram, in order to keep the capital–labour ratio constant. The dynamic response of employment and output to the rise in r thus looks as in Figure 5.4 but with no initial fall in Q and L. For an unanticipated permanent increase in the rate of interest, the opposite occurs.

(d) *The Constrained Firm*

Substituting for F_K/F_L, assuming a Cobb–Douglas technology, into (11), gives us the following pair of equations of motion which summarize the first-order conditions for the constrained firm:

$$\dot{\mu} = \mu(r + \delta) - \frac{\alpha}{1-\alpha} w \left(\frac{\bar{Q}}{K}\right)^{1/(1-\alpha)} \tag{14}$$

$$\dot{K} = I(\mu) - \delta K. \tag{10b}$$

Derived from a cost minimization model, it is this case that Abel concentrates on. The phase diagram is shown in Figure 5.6. The $\dot{K} = 0$ locus is exactly as before. The $\dot{\mu} = 0$ locus is now downward-sloping, since along the $\dot{\mu} = 0$ locus

$$\mu(r + \delta) = \frac{\alpha}{1-\alpha} w \left(\frac{\bar{Q}}{K}\right)^{1/(1-\alpha)}$$

and thus as K increases μ must fall to maintain the equality. Again, the system has a saddlepoint solution with arrows of motion as drawn where in this case the stable path is downward-sloping.

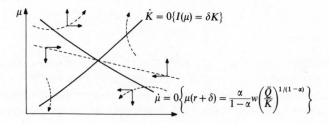

Figure 5.6

Consider for the constrained firm the effect at time t_0 of an unanticipated permanent increase in the wage rate. The $\dot{K} = 0$ locus is unaffected and the $\dot{\mu} = 0$ locus is shifted up. This phase diagram therefore is as shown in Figure 5.7.

The firm is initially in steady state, doing replacement investment sufficient to maintain the capital stock K^*. Following the increase in the wage rates, the only path that leads to the new steady state with no future jumps in μ is the new stable path. Thus μ jumps instantaneously to $\mu(t_0)$ and thereafter moves down the stable path. The time paths of investment and capital stock therefore are as shown in Figure 5.8.

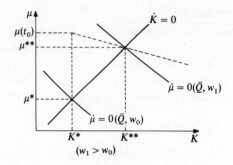

Figure 5.7

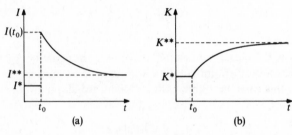

Figure 5.8

Investment therefore initially jumps (to $I(t_0)$), thus overshooting the long-run steady-state level, and then gradually falls to I^{**} $(>I^*)$. Since the phase diagram is drawn under the assumption that the firm is always demand-constrained and thus is always producing output $\bar{Q}$, it is straightforward, knowing the time path of K, to deduce the time path for employment.

The cases of changes in the level of demand and the rate of interest are equally straightforward and qualitatively the same as the change in the wage rate examined above. It suffices therefore to say that an increase in the level of demand shifts the $\dot{\mu} = 0$ locus upward, as does a fall in the rate of interest.

3 Switching between Regimes: A Unified Analysis of Cost Minimization and Profit Maximization Models of the Firm

The above analysis clearly draws attention to the possibility of regime-switching—in that a previously unconstrained firm becomes demand-constrained or vice versa—in two senses. First, and most straightforward, a firm that was demand-constrained may immediately become unconstrained and remain so. The second and more interesting case is the possibility that, for falls in the rate of interest and wage rate at some initial date t, the firm is initially unconstrained, but that, because of the desired gradual increase in output in response to such changes, the firm will, at some later date t', find itself facing a sales constraint. Given rational expectations, which in this deterministic model imply perfect foresight, the firm must anticipate this, and it is primarily with how this will affect the firm decisions that we are concerned.

Conversely, a firm that initially faces a sales constraint may experience a change in wage rate or rate of interest which, although still leaving it demand-constrained in the short run, may mean that the firm must anticipate, as desired output falls, that it becomes unconstrained.

Given the relatively large fluctuations in relative prices and aggregate demand that have taken place in the last decade, the unified treatment of which for the goods and labour market was an important part of Malinvaud (1977), it is important that investment theory incorporates the above possibility of firms switching between regimes.

(a) The Initially Constrained Firm: An Increase in the Level of Demand from $\bar{Q}_0$ to $\bar{Q}_1$

We consider first an increase in the level of demand at time t_0 large enough to leave a constrained firm unconstrained at all future dates. This has two advantages: first, it is the simplest case of regime-switching to analyse; second, being just a special case of the more general analysis, it allows us to progress gradually to the more complex general case.

Assume, then, that the firm is initially in steady state and is demand-constrained. If the unanticipated permanent change in demand from $\bar{Q}_0$ to $\bar{Q}_1$ occurs at time t_0, after which the firm is always unconstrained, then the sets of equation of motions which hold are:

for $t < t_0$:

$$\left. \begin{array}{l} \dot{\mu}(t) = \mu(t)(r + \delta) - \dfrac{\alpha}{1 - \alpha} w \left\{ \dfrac{\bar{Q}_0}{K(t)} \right\}^{1/(1 - \alpha)} \\[3mm] \dot{K}(t) = I\{\mu(t)\} - \delta K(t) \end{array} \right\} \qquad (15)$$

and for $t \geqslant t_0$:

$$\dot{\mu}(t) = \mu(t)(r + \delta) - p\alpha\left(\frac{1}{1-\alpha}\frac{w}{p}\right)^{(\alpha-1)/\alpha}$$

$$\dot{K}(t) = I\{\mu(t)\} - \delta K(t). \tag{16}$$

The full response of investment can be represented in a phase diagram that simply combines those in Section 2 (Figure 5.9).

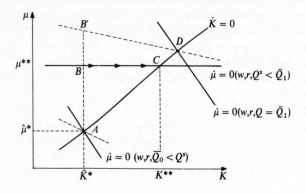

Figure 5.9

Following the increase in demand, the behaviour of (μ, K) is governed by the equations of motion (16). Anticipated jumps in μ are, for reasons given in Chapter 3, ruled out. Thus, μ must jump instantaneously to B on the new stable path and the firm will move along BC thereafter. From the discussion of Section 2, we can deduce the behaviour of output and employment along such a path. From the marginal productivity of labour condition, the capital–labour ratio before the demand change is given by

$$(p - \lambda)F_L(\cdot) = w$$

and so

$$\frac{K}{L} = \left(\frac{w}{p-\lambda}\frac{1}{1-\alpha}\right)^{1/\alpha} \quad t < t_0.$$

After the demand change, the captial–labour ratio is given by

$$pF_L(\cdot) = w$$

and so

$$\frac{K}{L} = \left(\frac{w}{p}\frac{1}{1-\alpha}\right)^{1/\alpha} \quad t \geqslant t_0.$$

Since $\lambda > 0$ because the firm is initially demand-constrained, it is clear that, instantaneously, the capital–labour ratio falls, after which time it remains constant. With K unchanged instantaneously, the firm must immediately take on more labour and produce more output. Output and employment then grow steadily in line with the capital stock, keeping the capital–labour ratio constant (see Figure 5.10).

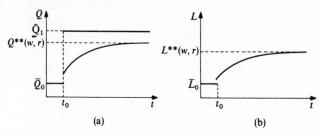

Figure 5.10

The important point to note is, as we found in Section 2, the gradual adjustment of output and employment to their new steady-state values, even though the firm becomes completely unconstrained immediately.

This, then, is the first and most obvious case of a firm that switches regimes from being constrained to being unconstrained, and for purposes of comparison we can briefly illustrate the results that would have followed from the pure cost minimization model. The $\dot{\mu} = 0$ locus for a firm producing $\bar{Q}_1 > Q^{**}(w, r)$, where $Q^{**}(\cdot)$ is the steady-state level of output that would be produced by a profit-maximizing firm, must intersect the $\dot{K} = 0$ locus at a point such as D in Figure 5.9, since the firm will require a higher steady-state level of K (and L) to produce the higher output. Thus the downward-sloping stable path for the cost minimization model lies everywhere above BC. Under cost minimization, μ would jump to a point such as B' and the firm would then move along $B'D$. The different paths of investment and capital stock of the cost minimization and regime-switching (profit maximization) models would look like Figure 5.11.

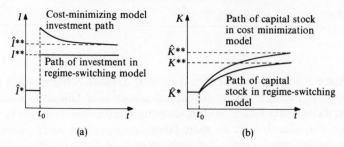

Figure 5.11

The above is reasonably straightforward because, although the firm switches regimes, it becomes immediately unconstrained following the unanticipated change in demand. We shall now use this to analyse the intermediate case of an increase in demand that relaxes the demand constraint but still leaves the firm constrained in the steady state. Consider then the case of an unanticipated permanent increase in the level of demand from $\bar{Q}_0$ to $\bar{Q}_2$, as in Figure 5.12.

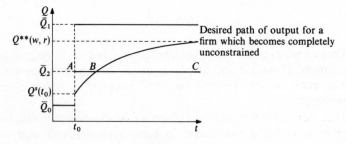

Figure 5.12

The path ABC for output is by definition that which the cost-minimizing firm would follow. However, this is not the path of output that would be chosen by a profit-maximizing firm. To follow ABC would be to produce more output initially than would a firm that became totally unconstrained. Such a path is less profitable and will not be chosen. To see this, look at the marginal productivity condition for labour. For the completely unconstrained firm, at the instant demand increases (to $\bar{Q}_1$, say, in the previous example), more labour will be taken on and output produced *until* the marginal product of labour equals the real wage; that is, Q and L are increased until

$$\frac{w}{p} = MP_L = (1-\alpha)\left(\frac{Q}{K}\right)^{-\alpha/(1-\alpha)} = (1-\alpha)\left\{\left(\frac{Q}{K}\right)^{\alpha/(1-\alpha)}\right\}^{-1}$$

and so, at t_0,

$$\frac{w}{p} = (1-\alpha)\left[\frac{\{Q^s(t_0)\}^{\alpha/(1-\alpha)}}{K(t_0)}\right]^{-1}.$$

Since $K(t_0)$ is predetermined, to instantaneously produce a greater level of output ($\bar{Q}_2$, say) than would a firm that was unconstrained ($Q^s(t_0)$) would drive down the marginal product of labour below the real wage. Profits could clearly be increased by taking on less labour and producing a lower level of output. This argument also tells us that, even if the firm expects to become demand-constrained in the future (as it must if demand is $\bar{Q}_2$), the output produced at t_0 will nevertheless be $Q^s(t_0)$—the same as a firm that expects no such demand constraint.

With demand $\bar{Q}_2$ and, from the preceding argument, initial output of $Q^s(t_0)$, we know that the firm is initially unconstrained and so the system is governed by the following equations of motion:

$$\left.\begin{aligned}
\dot{\mu} &= \mu(r+\delta) - p\alpha\left(\frac{1}{1-\alpha}\frac{w}{p}\right)^{(\alpha-1)/\alpha} \\
\dot{K} &= I(\mu) - \delta K.
\end{aligned}\right\} \tag{17}$$

But the firm must anticipate becoming demand-constrained, when behaviour will be determined by the following equations of motion:

$$\left.\begin{aligned}
\dot{\mu} &= \mu(r+\delta) - \frac{\alpha}{1-\alpha}w\left(\frac{\bar{Q}_2}{K}\right)^{1/(1-\alpha)} \\
\dot{K} &= I(\mu) - \delta K.
\end{aligned}\right\} \tag{18}$$

The final piece of information needed to be able to draw the phase diagram that can represent regime-switching is *when* the firm expects to become demand-constrained. In terms of the phase diagram, the relevant question is, At what level of the capital stock does the constraint begin to bite? Again, this can be deduced from the marginal productivity of labour condition. If the firm is unconstrained,

$$F_L(\cdot) = \frac{w}{p};$$

that is,

$$(1-\alpha)\left(\frac{Q}{K}\right)^{-\alpha/(1-\alpha)} = \frac{w}{p}.$$

Thus, when the firm is just about to become constrained with demand $\bar{Q}_2$,

$$(1-\alpha)\left(\frac{\bar{Q}_2}{\hat{K}}\right)^{-\alpha/(1-\alpha)} = \frac{w}{p}$$

where $\hat{K}$ = the capital stock at which the firm just becomes constrained.

For $K < \hat{K}$, the marginal product of labour is less than the real wage and a profit-maximizing firm would cut back on output and employment. For $K > \hat{K}$, the marginal product of labour is greater than the real wage and a profit-maximizing firm would expand output beyond $\bar{Q}_2$ and take on more labour.

It will be useful in what follows to recognize that the capital stock at which the demand constraint becomes binding is also given by the intersection of the constrained and unconstrained $\dot{\mu} = 0$ loci (point B' in Figure 5.13).[2]

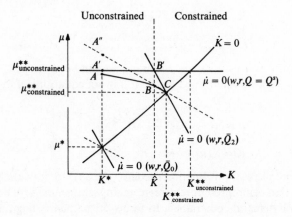

Figure 5.13

The full phase diagram can now be drawn and is shown in Figure 5.13. The optimal path, ABC, is constructed as follows. We know that initially the firm is unconstrained and μ, K are therefore driven by equations of motion (17). We also know that at capital stock $\hat{K}$ the firm becomes demand-constrained and remains so. Thus, for all $K > \hat{K}$ the firm must be moving down the stable path corresponding to equations of motion (18). An obvious path that satisfies the above requirements is $A'B'BC$. In this case, the unconstrained path is followed exactly until the sales constraint is hit, in which case output would follow the path OXY (see Figure 5.14). Intuitively, this path seems to suggest inappropriate behaviour on the part of a firm that anticipates facing a future constraint since behaviour prior to the constraint biting is unaffected. And, indeed, this path can be ruled out by the requirement that there be no anticipated jumps in μ, as would be implied by the path $A'B'BC$ in Figure 5.13.

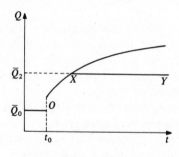

Figure 5.14

The exact path of (μ, K) is determined thus: μ jumps initially to such a level (A in Figure 5.13) that, when driven by the equations of motion (17) (the path AB), μ just hits the stable path corresponding to equations of motion (18) at capital stock $\hat{K}$ (B in the diagram). In this way, anticipated jumps in μ are ruled out. Thereafter (μ, K) are driven by equations of motion (18) (the path BC).

Not surprisingly, then, the level of investment undertaken by the firm can be seen to be lower at each moment. What we can also see is the full dynamic response of the firm and so we can see precisely how demand constraints affect the firm. In particular, we have noted that firms do not in general switch immediately from being constrained to being unconstrained or vice versa the moment the level of demand changes, since output, capital, and employment only gradually adjust to their future values. At all times, however, the behaviour of these variables is influenced by the anticipation of the sales constraint. The

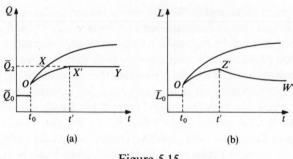

Figure 5.15

paths that output and employment follow are $OX'Y$ and $OZ'W'$ in Figure 5.15.

From time t_0 to t' the firm is unconstrained, which means, from the marginal productivity of labour condition, that the capital–labour ratio is unchanging. We know from earlier that, just at t_0, the firm takes on as much labour and produces the same output as the completely unconstrained firm. Since, from the phase diagram, the firm that expects to be demand-constrained makes less investment at each moment, the capital stock must grow less quickly and so, to keep the K/L ratio constant, output and employment must grow less quickly. Once the demand constraint is hit (at t'), output obviously remains at $\bar{Q}_2$ while the capital stock is still growing, although at a decreasing rate, and so employment must fall.

For the purpose of comparison, the path $A''BC$—which is the path μ, K would follow in the traditional cost-minimizing theory of the firm—is also drawn in Figure 5.13. μ jumps initially to a higher level (A'' rather than A) because the cost-minimizing firm initially produces a higher level of output ($\bar{Q}_2$ rather than $Q^s(t_0)$). For all $t < t'$, then, the cost-minimizing firm is producing a higher level of output than is required by profit maximization. To see precisely why this implies a higher value of μ, consider t_0 when demand has just increased to $\bar{Q}_2$. Since $K(t_0)$ is predetermined, the higher level of output can be produced only by taking on more labour, thereby driving down the marginal product of labour and pushing up the marginal product of capital. Hence the returns to capital must be larger. As capital is then substituted for labour (the firm continues to produce $\bar{Q}_2$ and K is growing), μ falls until eventually at B in the phase diagram both cost-minimizing and profit-maximizing firms have the same capital stock and are producing the same level of output and hence have the same μ. Again, a failure to allow for the possibility of regime-switching would have led to an over-prediction of the rate of investment.

The analysis presented here can be seen as a further progression in the illustration of models incorporating rational expectations. Early papers in this literature (e.g. Dornbusch 1976) used phase diagrams to analyse the dynamic implications of once-and-for-all unanticipated changes in variables affecting the behaviour of the system. The technique is now well known: in response to the change, the behaviour of the system is immediately governed by the new equations of motion. The new steady-state and saddlepoint solutions are calculated, and μ (or whichever relevant jump variable) jumps immediately to the new stable path and moves along it to the new steady state. In an important paper, Wilson (1979) subsequently generalized the analysis to show how phase diagrams could be used to illustrate the dynamic implications of changes in variables that are anticipated to occur at some known future date. In this literature, at time t_0 news hits the system of a change that will occur at time T ($> t_0$). New equations of motion will therefore determine the behaviour of the system from date T onwards, but $\forall t_0 \leqslant t < T$ the old equations of motion are relevant. The path of μ (say) is such that, prior to T, μ, driven by the old equations of motion, moves so as just to hit the newly relevant stable path at T. In this way anticipated jumps in μ are avoided.

The work of this Chapter can be seen as a nice varation on this analysis of anticipated changes. In this case, the news is of an unanticipated exogenous change taking place *immediately* (an increase in the level of demand), with the firm calculating that there will be a change of regime when new equations of motion become relevant. One way of putting this would be to say that anticipations of new equations of motion becoming relevant are endogenous. Rather than the time T at which the new stable path must be reached being exogenously specified, in this case the new stable path must be hit at a particular value of the predetermined variable (in this case K) and the 'time of arrival' is endogenous.

Very similar results to those above are obtained when considering the behaviour of firms that are initially unconstrained in response to a fall in both the wage rate and the rate of interest. The case of a fall in the wage rate (which is unanticipated and assumed to be permanent) is quickly illustrated.

Assume that the firm is initially unconstrained. From earlier we know that the wage rate change will cause the unconstrained firm to behave as in Fig. 5.16. If the level of demand is given by $\bar{Q}$ in Figure 5.16, then clearly the fall in the wage rate will be such as to leave the firm constrained at some future date.

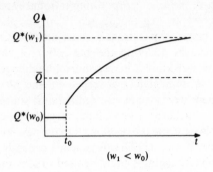

$(w_1 < w_0)$

Figure 5.16

By the same arguments as before, the firm will be initially unconstrained but as desired output grows the firm will hit the sales constraint. As before, then, the structure of the problem is that the behaviour of the firm is governed first by one set of equations of motion while unconstrained:

$$\left.\begin{aligned}\dot{\mu} &= \mu(r+\delta) - p\alpha\left(\frac{1}{1-\alpha}\frac{w_1}{p}\right)^{(\alpha-1)/\alpha}\\\dot{K} &= I(\mu) - \delta K\end{aligned}\right\} \tag{19}$$

and, when demand-constrained, by another set of equations of motion:

$$\left.\begin{aligned}\dot{\mu} &= \mu(r+\delta) - \frac{\alpha}{1-\alpha}w_1\left(\frac{\bar{Q}}{K}\right)^{1/(1-\alpha)}\\\dot{K} &= I(\mu) - \delta K.\end{aligned}\right\} \tag{20}$$

As before, the capital stock, $\hat{K}$, at which the firm just becomes demand-constrained is given by the intersection of the constrained and unconstrained $\dot{\mu} = 0$ loci. The appropriate phase diagram is very much as before (see Figure 5.17). Over AB the movement of (μ, K) is governed by equations of motion (19). At B, the firm just becomes demand-constrained and over BC, the path of (μ, K) is determined by

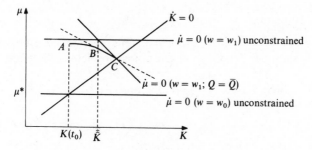

Figure 5.17

equations of motion (20). The initial jump in μ is such that there are no anticipated jumps in μ, and thus μ jumps to A so that, driven by (19), it just hits the constrained stable path at B. Output and employment follow the same kind of path as in the previous case.

Exactly the same analysis can be applied to the case of an unanticipated permanent fall in the rate of interest. The only difference in this case is that, as we have seen, there will be no anticipated jump in output and so the path for output will look like that shown in Figure 5.18.

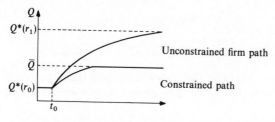

Figure 5.18

4 Employment Constraints

To continue the disequilibrium analysis of investment, we turn briefly to the case of employment constraints. These could be of the form either that the firm is unable to get rid of all the employees it wishes (a minimum constraint) or that it is unable to hire all the labour it requires (a maximum constraint). In Chapter 4 we saw that, as with demand and investment constraints, this causes marginal and average 'q' to diverge. In this section we shall look at the dynamics of the optimal investment behaviour of the firm, given possible employment constraints.

We consider the case of a maximum constraint on employment. From Section 3, the firm's optimization problem is therefore

$$\max V(t) = \int_t^\infty \Big\langle p(s) F\{K(s), L(s)\} - w(s)L(s)$$

$$- [I(s) + C\{I(s)\}] \Big\rangle \exp\{-r(s-t)\} ds$$

Subject to $\qquad \dot{K}(t) = I(t) - \delta K(t)$

$$L(t) \leqslant \bar{L}. \tag{21}$$

The Hamiltonian is

$$H = pF(K, L) - wL - \{I + C(I)\} + \mu(I - \delta K) + \lambda_L(\bar{L} - L) \tag{22}$$

with first-order conditions

$$\frac{d}{dt}(\mu e^{-rt}) = -\frac{\partial H e^{-rt}}{\partial K} \Rightarrow \dot{\mu} = \mu(r + \delta) - p F_K(\cdot) \tag{23}$$

$$\frac{\partial H}{\partial I} = 0 \Rightarrow \mu = 1 + C'(I) \tag{24}$$

$$\frac{\partial H}{\partial L} = 0 \Rightarrow p F_L(\cdot) = w + \lambda_L \tag{25}$$

$$\lambda_L(\bar{L} - L) = 0; \quad \lambda_L \geqslant 0. \tag{26}$$

Equation (24) says that investment is an increasing function of μ, which, using (23), is the ratio of the shadow price of capital goods

$$\mu_t = \int_t^\infty p F_K(s) \exp\{-(r + \delta)(s - t)\} ds$$

and the market price of those goods, here assumed to be unity, i.e. marginal 'q'. Equation (26) says that $\lambda_L > 0$ when the firm is employment-constrained, in which case, from (25), the marginal product of labour is greater than the real wage.

There are two cases to consider. The first is where the labour constraint does not bite and so the firm is unconstrained. We have now studied in detail the behaviour of the unconstrained firm and so we do no more than state that the equations describing the behaviour of the firm are given by (23), (24), and (25) with $\lambda_L = 0$, which imply the equations of motion (9b), (13) given the constant-returns-to-scale Cobb–Douglas assumption.

The second case is where the labour constraint does bind ($\lambda_L > 0$), in which case the equations of motion for the constrained firm are, after a little manipulation,

$$\dot{\mu} = \mu(r+\delta) - p\alpha\left(\frac{1}{1-\alpha}\frac{w+\lambda_L}{p}\right)^{(\alpha-1)/\alpha} \tag{27}$$

$$\dot{K} = I(\mu) - \delta K. \tag{9b}$$

A phase diagram can straightforwardly be constructed. Along the $\dot{\mu} = 0$ locus,

$$\mu(r+\delta) = p\alpha\left(\frac{1}{1-\alpha}\frac{w+\lambda_L}{p}\right)^{(\alpha-1)/\alpha}$$

We can see therefore that the effect of the labour constraint upon steady-state μ is to act like an increase in the money wage rate. Since $\lambda_L > 0$, the $\dot{\mu} = 0$ locus is shifted downwards compared with the unconstrained case. We can also deduce the slope of the $\dot{\mu} = 0$ locus. Along this locus,

$$\mu = \frac{1}{r+\delta}\,p\,F_K(\cdot) = \frac{1}{r+\delta}\,p\alpha\left(\frac{K}{\bar{L}}\right)^{\alpha-1}$$

and so

$$\left.\frac{d\mu}{dK}\right|_{\dot{\mu}=0} = \frac{1}{r+\delta}\,p\alpha\left(\frac{K}{\bar{L}}\right)^{\alpha-1}(\alpha-1)K^{-1} < 0.$$

Thus the $\dot{\mu} = 0$ locus for the employment-constrained firm is downward-sloping. Since the $\dot{K} = 0$ locus is as before, the complete phase diagram looks like Figure 5.19.

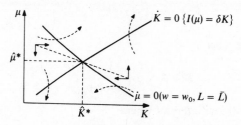

Figure 5.19

We shall now briefly consider the case of an *unanticipated permanent fall in the wage rate*. From Section 3 we know that this shifts the unconstrained $\dot{\mu} = 0$ locus upwards, leading to the response of output and employment shown in Figure 5.20. At t_0, following the change in wage rate, there is a once-and-for-all change (fall) in the K/L ratio which, for a given capital stock, implies a jump in employment and output. Thereafter the equations of motion tell us that the capital–labour ratio remains constant, which, since K is growing, implies that employment and output must be increasing as indicated.

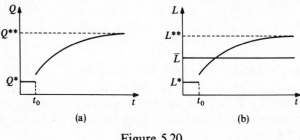

Figure 5.20

Now suppose that there is a labour constraint and the firm can obtain only an amount of labour $\bar{L}$. Then, as previously, we know that the firm will initially be unconstrained but will subsequently become constrained, and its actions will be influenced by this expectation. Again, the trick that allows us to develop the full phase diagram describing this is the splicing together of the two sets of equations of motions and hence phase diagrams. This requires us to solve for the capital stock at which the firm just becomes constrained. This obviously occurs for any given $\bar{L}$ when $\lambda_L = 0$, that is, when

$$F_L(\cdot) = (1-\alpha)(K/\bar{L})^\alpha = \frac{w}{p}$$

and therefore where

$$K = \hat{K} = \bar{L}\left(\frac{1}{1-\alpha}\frac{w}{p}\right)^{1/\alpha}.$$

The two $\dot{\mu} = 0$ loci intersect where

$$\mu(r+\delta) - pF_K(\cdot)^{CD} = \mu(r+\delta) - pF_K(\cdot)^{UCD}$$

that is, where

$$p\alpha \left(\frac{K}{\bar{L}}\right)^{\alpha-1} = p\alpha \left(\frac{1}{1-\alpha}\frac{w}{p}\right)^{(\alpha-1)/\alpha}$$

which is where

$$K = \bar{L}\left(\frac{1}{1-\alpha}\frac{w}{p}\right)^{1/\alpha}$$

Thus, as perhaps expected, given our previous results, the capital stock at which the firm just becomes constrained is given by the intersection of the constrained and unconstrained $\dot{\mu} = 0$ loci. The phase diagram for the case above therefore is shown in Figure 5.21. (μ, K) follow the path *ABC*. Since the firm becomes constrained at capital stock $\hat{K}$ and remains so thereafter, the stable path leading to the constrained steady state must be reached at $\hat{K}$ in order to avoid anticipated jumps in μ. Therefore μ must jump initially to such an extent that, when driven by equations of motion (9), (μ, K) just hit B in Figure 5.21. For this to be possible, the initial jump in must be to a point below the unconstrained $\dot{\mu} = 0$ locus. Therefore the firm that is subject to such a labour constraint is always doing less investment than the unconstrained firm and the capital stock is therefore growing less quickly. Since on the unconstrained part of the path the capital–labour ratio is determined entirely by the real wage, if K is growing less quickly, then so too must employment and output. At capital stock $\hat{K}$ the firm is just constrained and $L = \bar{L}$. However, it can be seen from Figure 5.21 that net investment is still taking place with,

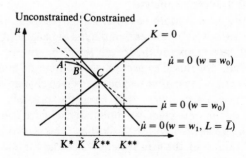

Figure 5.21

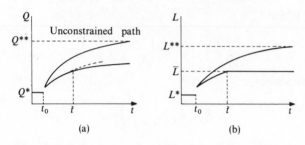

Figure 5.22

therefore, capital and output still growing. The time paths of output and employment therefore look like Figure 5.22 ($\tilde{t}$ is when the firm first becomes constrained).

5 Conclusion

In this chapter we have extended a popular model of the firm to incorporate the possibility of disequilibrium, and hence regime-switching, in both the labour and the product markets. In the latter case, by showing how to analyse the behaviour of a firm that faces the possibility of rationing, we have provided a unification of the two polar cases—the cost minimization and profit maximization approaches—which have dominated the neoclassical literature on investment. Increasingly, emphasis is placed on the importance of investment both in the short run, as an influence upon aggregate demand, and in the longer term, as a provider of productive capacity. The use of phase diagrams has allowed us to consider both aspects by providing a full dynamic analysis.

Although the main concern has been with investment, the analysis also allows us to look at output and employment behaviour and so is a quite general intertemporal theory of the firm. In the following chapter we shall use this background to examine in much greater detail the full variety of possible responses to given changes in demand and relative prices for a firm that faces the possibility of sales constraints. For the time being we note that exclusive concentration on either of the polar cases will be misleading. This is obvious enough where, as in Malinvaud, the firm switches once and for all from being demand-constrained to being unconstrained or vice versa. A quite wide range of intermediate cases, which also arise here, however, concerns the situation where a currently demand-constrained firm experiences an increase in demand which will leave it demand-constrained eventually but where the firm nevertheless becomes unconstrained immediately as it only gradually expands output and employment. To model this case as one of cost minimization would, despite the firm's eventually being demand-constrained, be misleading. Equally, although initially unconstrained, the firm's investment, output, and employment decisions are always affected by the knowledge that it will become demand-constrained. Analogous conclusions can be seen to hold for the case of employment constraints.

Finally, and more generally, this chapter has demonstrated, in the context of this extended '*q*' model, the possibility of using phase diagrams to analyse non-market-clearing rational expectations models. The general technique can be seen as an extension of that used in Wilson (1979).

Appendix   Proof that the Capital Stock at which the Demand Constraint Becomes Binding is Given by the Intersection of the Constrained and Unconstrained $\mu = 0$ loci

From (17) and (18), this is given by

$$p\alpha\left(\frac{1}{1-\alpha}\frac{w}{P}\right)^{(\alpha-1)/\alpha} = \frac{\alpha}{1-\alpha}w\left(\frac{\bar{Q}_2}{K}\right)^{1/(1-\alpha)}$$

and therefore

$$\frac{w}{p} = (1-\alpha)\left(\frac{\bar{Q}_2}{K}\right)^{-\alpha/(1-\alpha)}$$

as above.

The reason for this is clear. The value of μ along the $\dot{\mu} = 0$ locus tells us the present discounted value of a unit of capital assuming that the capital stock (and output and employment) remain constant: Along the constrained $\dot{\mu} = 0$ locus:

$$\mu\Big|_{\dot{\mu}=0} = \frac{\alpha}{1-\alpha}w\left(\frac{\bar{Q}}{K}\right)^{1/(1-\alpha)}\int_t^\infty \exp\{-(r+\delta)(s-t)\}ds$$

$$= \frac{1}{r+\delta}\frac{\alpha}{1-\alpha}w\left(\frac{\bar{Q}}{K}\right)^{1/(1-\alpha)}$$

Along the unconstrained $\dot{\mu} = 0$ locus:

$$\mu\bigg|_{\dot{\mu}=0} = \frac{\alpha}{1-\alpha}\, w \left(\frac{Q}{K}\right)^{1/(1-\alpha)} \int_t^\infty \exp\left\{-(r+\delta)(s-t)\right\}ds$$

$$= \frac{1}{r+\delta}\frac{\alpha}{1-\alpha}\, w \left(\frac{Q}{K}\right)^{1/(1-\alpha)}.$$

Since the Ks are the same, so too must be the Qs. Therefore the firm is just constrained.

Notes

1. I have already dealt with the more general case in Chapter 4 (see especially Appendix A for an explanation of the case presented here, i.e., intertemporal optimization subject to a possible sales constraint). We now use the first-order conditions derived to construct a phase diagram and analyse the decisions of the firm in detail.
2. I am grateful to Colin Mayer for pointing this out to me. See the Appendix to this chapter for proof.

6

Dynamic Adjustment with a Putty–Putty Technology: Demand and Relative Price Changes in an Integrated Model

1 Introduction

Since Jorgenson (1963), theoretical work on investment has typically assumed a putty–putty technology. In other words, capital is assumed to be as malleable *ex post* as it is *ex ante*. An alternative frequently proposed as more realistic is that of putty–clay, where the elasticity of substitution of capital for labour is smaller *ex post* than it is *ex ante*. In this tradition, as we saw in Chapter 1, the particular assumption often made is that the firm can choose capital with any desired capital–labour ratio *ex ante* but once installed the capital becomes hard baked clay: the *ex post* elasticity of substitution of capital for labour is zero.

In trying to arbitrate between the alternative technologies, the empirical finding that the capital stock responds more quickly to an increase in demand than to a change in relative prices has been put forward as evidence in favour of the putty–clay hypothesis (see, e.g., Bischoff 1971a, 1971b; Hausman 1973). However, a recent article by Abel (1981) draws attention to the need to exercise caution in the interpretation of such data by showing that the same relative speeds of response can be derived from the behaviour of an intertemporally optimizing firm with a putty–putty production function and subject to costs of adjustment.

In order to address the question of the relative speeds of response from a theoretical standpoint, it is, of course, necessary to have a model that admits the possibility of both demand and relative prices influencing investment. Consequently, as in Abel, the usual framework within which this question is posed is that of the cost-minimizing firm. However, this framework is unnecessarily restrictive since, given relative prices, there will be some levels of output which the firm will find it unprofitable to produce. In the previous chapter we saw how to integrate the cost minimization and profit maximization approaches to investment theory and so provide a unified analysis of the investment behaviour of the firm that faces the possibility of being demand-constrained, and hence of the special case of the cost-minimizing model being relevant. At the same time, it is recognized that the firm may choose not to increase production because it is unprofitable to do so. This chapter therefore reconsiders the question posed by Abel in a more general framework, which does not always assume that the firm simply minimizes the cost of meeting a given level of output.

Within the confines of the debate initiated by Abel, I shall show how, while it is true that the putty–putty model is capable of producing a faster response to demand changes than to relative price changes, it is also not difficult to reverse the ranking. My intention, however, is the more general one of illustrating how the integrated model of the firm produces an extremely rich menu of dynamic responses, and that *the range of possibilities that exist makes it impossible to draw any unambiguous conclusion about the relative speeds of response.*

The plan of the chapter is as follows. In Section 2 the basic argument of Abel is quickly rehearsed and I make some brief comments while retaining his assumption of cost minimization. In Section 3 I broaden the analysis by using the integrated model introduced in Chapter 5 to compare demand and relative price changes. While Abel considers a broad class of production functions, we need only examine the special case of the Cobb–Douglas in order to demonstrate the range of possible results. Greatest attention is given to the study of wage rate changes, since for this case the strongest contrast in result is possible. Section 4 looks at some of the implications of the results for policy evaluation and econometric model building, and Section 5 concludes.

2   The Response of the Constrained Firm to Demand and Relative Price Changes

The model is, as stated above, that of the previous chapter. It contains as a special case that of Abel, who examines the response of investment to demand and relative price changes in a cost-minimizing model where the path of output, $\bar{Q}$, is taken as exogenous. Hence $Q = \bar{Q}$ and the equations of motion are, as we saw in Chapter 5, always given by

$$\dot{\mu} = \mu(r+\delta) - w\frac{F_K(\cdot)}{F_L(\cdot)} \tag{1}$$

$$\dot{K} = I(\mu) - \delta K. \tag{2}$$

Assuming a constant-returns-to-scale Cobb–Douglas production function $K^\alpha L^{1-\alpha}$, (1) becomes

$$\dot{\mu} = \mu(r+\delta) - \frac{\alpha}{1-\alpha}w\left(\frac{\bar{Q}}{K}\right)^{1/(1-\alpha)} \tag{3}$$

which, combined with (2), can be used to construct the phase diagram in Figure 6.1. Because the diagram will be used in what follows, I shall quickly rehearse its explanation.

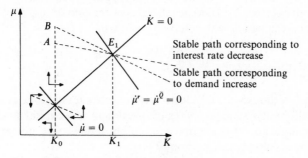

Figure 6.1

The $\dot{K} = 0$ locus is drawn upward-sloping since it is defined by $I(\mu) = \delta K$. μ must increase as K does in order to bring forth the higher investment required for depreciation. The $\dot{\mu} = 0$ locus is downward-sloping, being defined by

$$\mu(r+\delta) = \frac{\alpha}{1-\alpha}w\left(\frac{\bar{Q}}{K}\right)^{1/(1-\alpha)}$$

and hence, as K increases, μ must fall to maintain the equality. Briefly, the arrows of motion of the system are such that above the $\dot{K} = 0$ locus $I > \delta K$ and hence $\dot{K} > 0$ and the capital stock is growing. Above the $\dot{\mu} = 0$ locus,

$$\mu(r+\delta) > \frac{\alpha}{1-\alpha}w\left(\frac{\bar{Q}}{K}\right)^{1/(1-\alpha)}$$

and hence $\dot{\mu} > 0$ and μ is rising. The equations of motion are therefore as drawn in Figure 6.1, and it can be seen that the system has a saddlepoint solution with a unique downward-sloping stable path to equilibrium.

The basic argument of Abel is as follows. Consider changes in the rate of interest and level of demand which lead to the same steady-state capital stock, K_1. Thus, suppose there is an unanticipated permanent decrease in the interest rate which causes $(r + \delta)$ to fall to $(r + \delta)(1/\gamma)$ where $\gamma > 1$. This shifts up the $\dot{\mu} = 0$ locus as in Figure 6.1 with the new locus being given by

$$\mu(r + \delta)\frac{1}{\gamma} = \frac{\alpha}{1 - \alpha}w\left(\frac{\bar{Q}}{K}\right)^{1/(1 - \alpha)}. \tag{4}$$

Exactly the same increase in steady-state capital stock could of course have been obtained by increasing the level of demand from $\bar{Q}$ to $\gamma^{1-\alpha}\bar{Q}$ since then the new $\dot{\mu} = 0$ would be given by

$$\mu(r + \delta) = \frac{\alpha}{1 - \alpha}w\left(\gamma^{1-\alpha}\frac{\bar{Q}}{K}\right)^{1/(1 - \alpha)} = \gamma\frac{\alpha}{1 - \alpha}w\left(\frac{\bar{Q}}{K}\right)^{1/(1 - \alpha)}. \tag{4'}$$

However, although the effects on steady-state capital stock may be identical, the dynamic responses of investment and capital stock to these changes are different. In the case of the interest rate change, the equation of motion for μ becomes

$$\dot{\mu}^r = \mu(r + \delta)\frac{1}{\gamma} - \frac{\alpha}{1 - \alpha}w\left(\frac{\bar{Q}}{K}\right)^{1/(1 - \alpha)} \tag{5}$$

while for the demand increase we have

$$\dot{\mu}^{\bar{Q}} = \mu(r + \delta) - \gamma\frac{\alpha}{1 - \alpha}w\left(\frac{\bar{Q}}{K}\right)^{1/(1 - \alpha)}. \tag{5'}$$

Multiplying through by γ in (13), we can see that for any pair (μ, K)

$$\dot{\mu}^{\bar{Q}} = \gamma\dot{\mu}^r$$

and hence $\dot{\mu}^{\bar{Q}} > \dot{\mu}^r$ since $\gamma > 1$. This has the implication that, although the same long-run equilibrium, E_1, is reached, the unique stable path to steady state is steeper for a demand increase than for an interest rate decrease, as drawn in the figure. The reason for this is that, since $\dot{\mu}^{\bar{Q}} > \dot{\mu}^r$, the arrows of motion determining the behaviour of (μ, K) at a point to the north-west of E_1 are as in Figure 6.2. Thus, the vector of

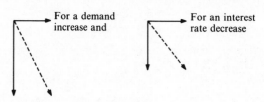

Figure 6.2

motion at a point to the north-west of E_1 slopes downward more steeply in the case of a demand increase than for an interest rate decrease. The net result is that the fall in r causes the system to jump to point A in Figure 6.1 while the increase in demand causes the system to jump to point B, where μ and hence investment are higher. Thus the initial jump in investment is larger and the system moves more quickly to the new steady state for a demand increase compared with an interest rate decrease, *resulting in the same steady state* which is a pattern of response suggested by the putty–clay hypothesis. By the same reasoning, it can be seen that an increase in the wage rate from w to γw leads to the same steady state as the changes considered above, and furthermore the dynamic response of investment is identical to that for the increase in demand.

Remaining in the cost-minimizing framework, we can still make some remarks about this result. First, it is only if net investment is positive that the above conclusions hold. Second, even if net investment is positive, for an exogenous change that *decreases* the steady-state capital stock, there is a sense in which an interest rate change produces a faster response than a demand or wage rate change. To see this consider the same proportionate changes in interest rate and demand from $(r + \delta)$ to $(r + \delta)(1/\gamma)$ and from $\bar{Q}$ to $\gamma^{1-\alpha}\bar{Q}$ but now let $\gamma < 1$. These changes therefore decrease the steady-state capital stock and as before $\mu^Q = \mu^r$, but this now implies that $\mu^Q < \mu^r$. Thus the stable path corresponding to the interest rate increase is steeper than that corresponding to the demand decrease. The phase diagram for this case is drawn in Figure 6.3.

It can be seen that, if the system was initially at rest at E_0, such changes would lead to negative net investment and μ would fall to points C' and B', respectively. The system would therefore react more quickly to the interest rate change than to the demand change. In order to consider positive net investment the system would initially

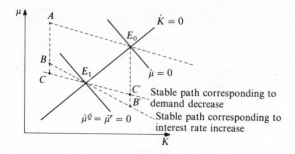

Figure 6.3

have to be out of steady state at a position such as *A*. Then μ falls immediately to *B* for the interest rate increase and to *C* for the demand decrease. Thus the immediate response of investment is greater in magnitude for the output change than for the interest rate change. However, the system will nevertheless reach the new steady state more quickly under the interest rate change. Thus the capital stock will react more quickly to the interest rate change than to the output change. Finally, there is an instantaneous reaction of the capital–labour ratio for the demand decrease since, given the capital stock, employment must be reduced. There is no immediate response of the capital–labour ratio to the interest rate change. In both cases, the capital–labour ratio then continually approaches the new long-run equilibrium level as the capital stock grows. This distinction between the response of investment, the capital stock, and capital–labour ratio has not always been clearly brought out (see also Nickell 1978 on this point), and so in what follows I shall outline the behaviour of each of these variables for the various changes considered.

3   A Unified Analysis of Demand and Relative Price Changes

In Chapter 5 I outlined the maximization problem of a firm for which the assumption of cost minimization is not always appropriate because not all levels of demand leave the firm demand-constrained. Given relative prices, there will be some levels of output that firms will find it unprofitable to produce. There will therefore be some changes in demand and relative prices which cause firms to switch from being demand-constrained to being unconstrained and vice versa. We shall now compare the responses of firms to exogenous changes within this framework in order to see how the conclusions change once the special case of cost minimization is generalized. For purposes of illustration we shall consider only the most straightforward cases of regime-switching, where firms move immediately from being demand-constrained to being unconstrained. The analysis is however quite general, as we have seen, and is capable of handling the more complex intermediate case of changes that leave the firm initially unconstrained but destined at some later date to hit a demand constraint as output is gradually expanded. In each of the examples that will be illustrated below we shall be assuming the same proportional increase in demand and wage rates (from $\bar{Q}$ to $\gamma^{1-\alpha}\bar{Q}$; w to γw) and decrease in interest rates (from $(r+\delta)$ to $\{(r+\delta)(1/\gamma)\}$).

The first case is the comparison of an interest rate change and demand increase where the latter is such as to leave the firm just unconstrained in the new steady state. To be more precise, the level of final demand, $\gamma^{1-\alpha}\bar{Q}$, is just sufficient to allow the firm to sell its desired (notional) steady-state output Q^{**}. The phase diagram for such a case looks like Figure 6.4.

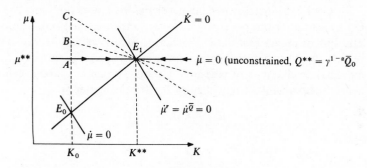

Figure 6.4

As described in the previous section, the equations of motion for μ of the cost-minimizing firm become

$$\dot{\mu}^r = \mu(r+\delta)_0 \frac{1}{\gamma} - \frac{\alpha}{1-\alpha} w \left(\frac{\bar{Q}_0}{K} \right)^{1/(1-\alpha)} \qquad (6a)$$

$$\dot{\mu}^{\bar{Q}} = \mu(r+\delta)_0 - \gamma \frac{\alpha}{1-\alpha} w \left(\frac{\bar{Q}_0}{K} \right)^{1/(1-\alpha)} \qquad (6b)$$

and so the corresponding $\dot{\mu} = 0$ locus shifts up with new steady state

E_1. μ jumps up to point C for the demand increase and point B for the interest rate decrease.

This, however, assumes that the firm always chooses to produce output equal to the given level of demand. In fact this is not so: as we know from the previous chapter, the firm immediately becomes unconstrained following the demand increase and *only gradually expands output to meet the increased demand*. Given the Cobb–Douglas assumption, the equations of motion that govern the behaviour of the firm therefore become

$$\dot{\mu} = \mu(r+\delta)_0 - p\alpha\left(\frac{1}{1-\alpha}\frac{w}{p}\right)^{(\alpha-1)/\alpha} \tag{7}$$

$$\dot{K} = I(\mu) - \delta K \tag{2}$$

with, as we know, a saddlepoint solution for the system where the unique stable path to long-run equilibrium E_1 is given by the unconstrained $\dot{\mu} = 0$ locus. We know the steady state is E_1 because the level of final demand $\gamma^{1-\alpha}\bar{Q}_0$ is by hypothesis just equal to the level of output the firm would choose to produce in steady state, Q^{**}.

Following the increase in demand, therefore, μ does not jump to C but instead jumps to point A on the new unconstrained stable path. The system moves along AE, thereafter. Again, we can deduce the behaviour of output and employment along such a path from the marginal productivity of labour condition. The capital–labour ratio before the demand change is given by (from Chapter 5)

$$(p-\lambda)F_L(\cdot) = w$$

and so

$$\frac{K}{L} = \left(\frac{w}{p-\lambda}\frac{1}{1-\alpha}\right)^{1/\alpha}. \tag{8}$$

After the demand change when the firm is unconstrained, $\lambda = 0$ and the capital–labour ratio is given by

$$pF_L(\cdot) = w$$

and so

$$\frac{K}{L} = \left(\frac{w}{p}\frac{1}{1-\alpha}\right)^{1/\alpha}. \tag{9}$$

Since $\lambda > 0$ because the firm is initially demand-constrained, it is clear that instantaneously the capital–labour ratio falls, after which time it ramains constant. With K unchanged, instantaneously the firm must immediately take on more labour and produce more output. Output and employment then grow steadily in line with the capital stock, keeping the capital–labour ratio constant. The time paths of output and employment, assuming that the demand change occurred at t_0, are given in Figure 6.5. In this case therefore demand increases from $\bar{Q}_0$ to $\gamma^{1-\alpha}\bar{Q}_0$ and the firm immediately becomes unconstrained but output does not immediately increase to $\gamma^{1-\alpha}\bar{Q}_0$.

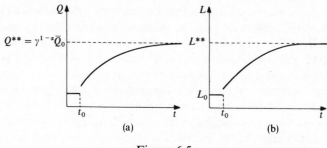

Figure 6.5

By contrast, a fall in the rate of interest not only changes the relative price of capital and labour, thereby causing a demand-constrained firm to substitute capital for labour and the constrained $\dot{\mu}^r = 0$ locus to shift upward to E_1, but it also increases the desired (notional) output of the firm. Consequently the unconstrained $\dot{\mu} = 0$ locus shifts upwards also and the firm *remains demand-constrained*. In fact, the extent of rationing has increased. The equations of motion of the cost-minimizing model therefore remain relevant, and μ does indeed jump to B in Figure 6.4.

One can see therefore that the conclusion about the speeds of response of investment and capital stock to changes in the interest rate and level of demand has been reversed. Here the reaction is larger and quicker for the fall in the interest rate. The reason for this is that, given initial prices (p,w,r) and capital stock (K_0), it is unprofitable to immediately begin producing output $\gamma^{1-\alpha}\bar{Q}_0$, as happens in the pure cost-minimizing model. To do so would be to produce more output and hence employ more labour than an unconstrained firm. Consequently this would not be profit-maximizing, since it would imply driving the marginal product of labour below the real wage. Since employment is lower than in the cost-minimizing model, so too is the marginal product of capital and hence μ and investment. Finally, for the demand increase there is an immediate once-and-for-all change (fall) in the capital–labour ratio while for the interest rate decrease there is no immediate reaction but the capital–labour ratio is continually changing (increasing) thereafter as the firm's capital stock grows.

More interesting, and more complex, possibilities arise when we include wage rate changes in the analysis. Consider a demand-constrained firm that is faced with an (unanticipated permanent) increase in wages. If the firm remains demand-constrained we know, from earlier chapters, that the increase in wage rates, by making capital a relatively cheap method of production of the given level of output, will increase investment. However, we also know that an increase in the wage rate reduces the desired output of the firm and raises the possibility that the demand-constrained firm becomes unconstrained. In such a circumstance not only would a failure to take account of regime-switching overestimate the response of investment, but it may also predict exactly the wrong direction for investment. This emphasizes a general conclusion we have in fact seen earlier: that, in order to be able to predict the full dynamic response of the firm, one must know the initial conditions under which it operates. To demonstrate this fully we now present three different cases where the change in the wage rate is the same in each case but different initial conditions lead to very varied responses by the firm. Only for the first case will we compare the response with that of a demand change leading to the same steady state.

Case 1

We first consider a wage rate increase for an initially demand-constrained firm which again leaves the firm just unconstrained in steady state. The initial level of demand $\bar{Q}_0$ is therefore equal to the steady-state output that the firm wishes to produce following the wage rate increase from w_0 to γw_0. The phase diagram is drawn in Figure 6.6.

An increase in wage rates has two effects in the diagram. On the one hand, by making capital cheap relative to labour, firms are led to substitute capital for labour in the production of any given level of output. The cost-minimizing $\dot{\mu} = 0$ locus[1] therefore shifts up, leading to a higher steady-state capital stock K^{**}. On the other hand, the

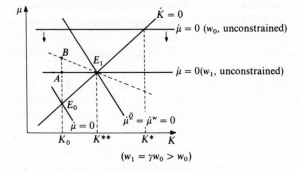

$$(w_1 = \gamma w_0 > w_0)$$

Figure 6.6

increase in wage rates will cause the firm to want to produce less output and so use less capital as profitability is lower. This is demonstrated by a downward shift in the unconstrained $\dot{\mu} = 0$ locus. From the previous chapter, since the constrained and unconstrained $\dot{\mu} = 0$ loci intersect to the right of K_0, we know that the firm immediately becomes unconstrained following the wage rate increase. μ therefore jumps to point A in the diagram and thereafter remains constant. The full response of the firm is illustrated in Figure 6.7.

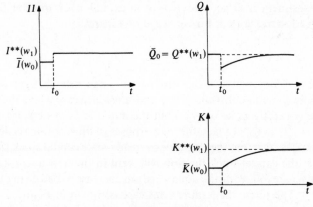

Figure 6.7

Since μ jumps from E_0 to A in the phase diagram, this tells us that investment also jumps and remains constant thereafter. Since the firm immediately becomes unconstrained, we know that the capital–labour ratio is constant $\forall t > t_0$. K is growing, and thus Q and L must be growing at the same rate. Since demand is unchanged at $\bar{Q}_0$, which, by construction, is just the level of output to be produced in steady state, this means that output must fall instantaneously and rise steadily after t_0.

Comparing this relative price change to a demand increase that leads to the same steady state, we can see that such a change will leave the firm still demand-constrained in steady state with the equation of motion for μ therefore given by

$$\dot{\mu} = \mu(r+\delta)_0 - \gamma \frac{\alpha}{1-\alpha} w_0 \left(\frac{\bar{Q}_0}{K}\right)^{1/(1-\alpha)}. \tag{10}$$

We know this because the new steady-state capital stock K^{**} is less than K^*, the steady-state capital stock an unconstrained firm would choose, faced with wage rate and interest rate w_0, $(r+\delta)_0$.

One can see therefore that for the wage increase μ jumps to point A in the diagram, while for the demand increase μ jumps to point B.[2] In this case therefore the speed of response of the system is no longer the same for wage rate and demand increases, as Abel found in looking at a cost-minimizing model of the firm. For changes in these variables that lead to the same steady state, we see that the putty–putty model is, in fact, capable of giving a putty–clay type response. The initial jump in investment is larger and growth in capital stock quicker for the demand increase than for the wage rate increase.

Case 2

We now continue with our analysis of wage rate changes for the initially demand-constrained firm and consider a case where the initial wage is exactly as before (w_0) but the initial level of demand, $\bar{Q}_1$, is higher $(\bar{Q}_1 > \bar{Q}_0)$. In fact, for the purposes of illustration, the level of demand is such that the constrained steady-state capital stock $(\bar{K}(w_0))$ is just the capital stock the firm will want in the new unconstrained steady state following the same wage rate increase as before $(w_0$ to $\gamma w_0 = w_1)$. The phase diagram for this case is shown in Figure 6.8.

The behaviour of investment, output, and capital stock is shown in Figure 6.9, where, for purposes of comparison, we also show what would have happened following the wage rate increase to a firm for which there was no demand constraint operating and which was therefore initially unconstrained with capital stock, $K^*(w_0)$. $I^*(w_0)$,

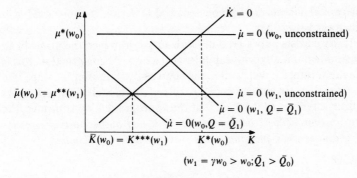

Figure 6.8

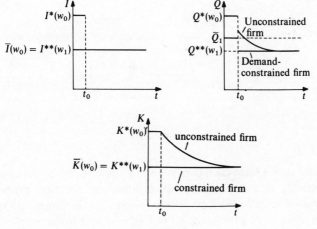

Figure 6.9

$Q^*(w_0), K^*(w_0) \equiv$ initial (steady state) investment, output, and capital stock of an unconstrained firm; $\bar{I}(w_0), \bar{Q}_1, \bar{K}(w_0) \equiv$ initial (steady-state) investment, output, and capital stock of a demand-constrained firm.

For an unconstrained firm an increase in the wage rate reduces desired capital stock, output, and investment and the unconstrained $\dot{\mu} = 0$ locus shifts down. As described in Chapter 5, there will be a once-and-for-all drop in investment and an immediate increase in the capital–labour ratio as labour is shed and output reduced. Thereafter, the capital–labour ratio is constant and Q, K, and L move gradually downwards together.

If there exists only a level of demand $\bar{Q}_1$, however, the firm will be constrained initially with capital stock $\bar{K}(w_0)$. By construction, this is the capital stock it will want in the new steady state after the wage rate increase to w_1. In consequence, because in this model adjustment costs attach only to capital, which is at the appropriate long-run value, the firm *instantaneously adjusts employment and output to their steady-state values while investment remains completely unchanged.*

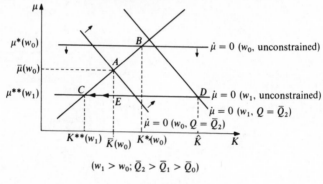

$$(w_1 > w_0; \bar{Q}_2 > \bar{Q}_1 > \bar{Q}_0)$$

Figure 6.10

Case 3

Consider now a third case, depicted in Figure 6.10, where the level of demand $\bar{Q}_2$ is still higher while still leaving the firm demand-constrained initially. With no demand constraint, the firm would be in steady state at B, producing output $Q^*(w_0)$ and doing investment $I^*(w_0)$. In fact, the level of demand $\bar{Q}_2$ is less than $Q^*(w_0)$ and so the firm is at A, with a lower capital stock, $\bar{K}(w_0)$ and level of investment $\bar{I}(w_0)$. The rise in the wage rate shifts down the $\dot{\mu} = 0$ locus of the unconstrained firm and shifts up the $\dot{\mu} = 0$ locus of the firm constrained always to produce output $\bar{Q}_2$. We are interested in knowing whether this leaves the firm constrained or unconstrained. This is straightforwardly decided as before by asking at what capital stock the firm would become constrained following such a change. This, as we know, is given by the intersection of the constrained and unconstrained $\dot{\mu} = 0$ loci—point D in the diagram. Therefore, as one might expect, given cases 1 and 2, the firm immediately becomes unconstrained following the wage rate increase; μ drops instantaneously to E in the diagram and (μ, K) move along EC on the new stable path thereafter. The behaviour of investment, output, and capital stock are shown in Figure 6.11, where we again compare this with the behaviour of an unconstrained firm.

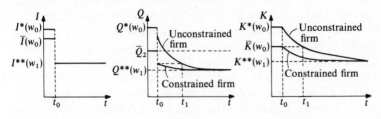

Figure 6.11

It can now be seen more clearly precisely why the firm becomes unconstrained immediately. Following the increase in wage rates, an unconstrained firm wishes to reduce output, investment, and capital stock to the new steady-state levels $Q^{**}(w_1)$, $I^{**}(w_1)$, and $K^{**}(w_1)$. The firm will therefore be unconstrained in steady state since $\bar{Q}_2 > Q^{**}(w_1)$. However, costly adjustment prevents the firm from immediately moving to its steady-state values, and output, employment, and capital stock are only gradually adjusted. The firm that was initially demand-constrained, however, had a lower initial capital stock, $\bar{K}(w_0)$. At t_1 the initially unconstrained firm would have capital stock $\bar{K}(w_0)$, and we can read off the desired path of output and capital stock from this point. *This* is the path followed by our demand-constrained firm, which *starts* with capital stock $\bar{K}(w_0)$, and so output drops instantaneously from $\bar{Q}_0$ to the newly appropriate level.

In conclusion, the three cases presented here illustrate vividly the variety of response that is possible for any given change (in wage rates). Without knowing the initial conditions, which here means without knowing the extent of initial rationing, it is impossible to say whether any of output,[3] investment, or the capital stock will fall or rise in response to the change in wage rates, let alone what the size of the response in any given direction will be.

4 Policy Implications

The analysis in the previous section and Chapter 5 of the possibility of regime-switching by profit-maximizing firms in response to changes in the economic environment leads to some interesting observations. First, and most obvious, the appropriate policy to stimulate investment varies according to which regime holds, exactly as in Malinvaud. For an unconstrained firm, increasing demand has no effect while a higher level of demand increases investment for the constrained firm. On the assumption that the firm does not switch regimes, the most dramatic contrast occurs, again as in Malinvaud, for changes in wage rates. This is well known in the context of the polar cases of the profit-maximizing and cost-minimizing approaches, as outlined in Abel. Second, it is also pointed out by Blanchard and Sachs (1982) that, when the firm faces the possibility of demand constraints, marginal 'q' (μ) and average 'q', defined as the ratio of the stock market value of the firm to the replacement cost of capital, are not equal. We know from Chapter 4 that it is straightforward to generalize the result of Hayashi under these circumstances to show, assuming no taxes, that

$$\text{marginal '}q\text{'} = \frac{V_t}{p_t^I K_t} - \frac{\int_t^\infty \lambda(s) \bar{Q}(s) \exp\{-r(s-t)\}\, ds}{p_t^I K_t}$$

where V_t = stock market value at t

$p_t^I K_t$ = replacement cost of capital stock.

The above authors go on to argue that, if the firm is demand-constrained, then, for an increase in the real wage, marginal and average 'q' will move in opposite directions, with an increase in real wages reducing profitability and hence the stock market value of the firm while increasing the wage savings on an extra unit of capital and hence marginal 'q'. We have noted in this chapter that marginal 'q' may respond in a variety of ways to an increase in the real wage rate for an initially demand-constrained firm depending on the initial conditions. In the particular case where the firm *always* remains constrained, marginal 'q' will indeed always increase in response to an increase in real wages, but this need not be so once regime-switching is allowed for.

Third, not only are the effects on investment different according to the regime, but so are the effects on employment. Changes in wage rates move employment in the same direction for both constrained and unconstrained firms, but again, the long-run and dynamic responses of firms differ according to the regime. In Malinvaud it is argued that in the region of Keynesian unemployment, where both firms and households are constrained, an increase in real wages, by increasing real purchasing power, would increase aggregate demand and employment. In the intertemporal model of this chapter we can see that this has to be modified in two ways. Offsetting the beneficial effects of higher real wages on consumption demand is the reduction of employment that results from the substitution of capital for labour. On the other hand, account must be taken of the extra demand generated by this increased investment. This suggests that the major stimulus to aggregate demand when real wages are increased in Keynesian unemployment, if the firm remains in that regime, may be investment rather than consumption.

Fourth, the conclusions of the first and third paragraphs must be modified to take account of regime-switching. Once this is allowed for, we have seen the great variety of dynamic responses that can occur. For an initially constrained firm there are three possibilities following an increase in demand: (1) the firm may simply remain constrained; (2) it may become initially unconstrained but eventually hit the new level of demand and be constrained in steady state; or (3) it may just become completely unconstrained. In each case the response of investment is in the same direction but the exact response is different, as are the employment effects. Worse still is the case of a wage rate change for the initially constrained firm, where investment may increase, decrease, or remain unchanged following a given increase in wage rates. Similarly, the behaviour of output and employment differs in each of the three cases. For policy purposes, therefore, it is not sufficient simply to be able to observe whether the firm is demand-constrained or not: the extent of rationing must also be determined.

In a recent paper set in the context of the putty–putty/putty–clay debate, Abel (1981) showed, using a cost-minimizing version of the model of Chapter 5, that a putty–putty technology can give a putty–clay type result. Specifically, he showed that, with a constant-returns-to-scale production function, for changes in demand, wage rates, and interest rates that lead to the same long-run capital stock, the dynamic response of investment will be identical for the demand and wage rate changes while investment will respond more quickly to an increase in demand than to a fall in the interest rate. Using the more general model introduced in the previous chapter, which allows for regime-switching, we have seen in two examples how it is possible to reverse this result with an interest rate change leading to a faster response of investment than a demand change, which in turn can produce a quicker response for investment than a wage rate change. It should be clear from the results of the remainder of this chapter that in fact it is impossible to give any unambiguous ranking to the speeds of response of investment to demand and relative prices without carefully specifying the market conditions.

From this we can also see that, in the integrated model presented here, the appropriate basis of comparison is the sensitivity of investment and capital stock to *given* changes in demand and relative prices rather than to changes that *lead to the same steady state*. For instance, in some of the above cases, once the firm becomes unconstrained, investment is completely insensitive to changes in demand all of which lead to the same steady state. For policy purposes, the issue is not just a comparison of the paths of investment and capital stock for exogenous changes leading to the same steady state; one should also take account of the size of the changes in demand and relative prices producing any given investment path. This distinction only arises because, given relative prices, the firm will not find it profitable to produce certain levels of output. It is not relevant to the pure cost minimization model.

Finally, we consider the implications for current econometric practices. In his important critique of econometric models, Lucas (1976) argued that parameter estimates obtained under one policy regime will not necessarily be relevant to prediction under different policy regimes since agents' behaviour, given rational expectations, is determined in part by their perception of policy. A similar caution is necessary here. Since the responsiveness of investment to exogenous changes depends on market conditions, there is no reason to expect parameter estimates of, say, the lag structure relevant for investment expenditures to be a reliable guide to the behaviour of investment in different states of the economy. A given policy carried out under different market conditions will lead to possibly very different investment policies on the part of firms. A particular example we have encountered in this chapter is that measures to increase real wages may lead to increased investment if firms are demand-constrained while reducing investment if firms are unconstrained.

5 Conclusion

This chapter takes a new approach to the question of the responsiveness of a firm's investment expenditures to demand and relative price changes raised in a recent article by Abel in the context of the putty–putty versus putty–clay debate. He examines the dynamic response of investment of a neoclassical firm subject to costs of adjustment in order to argue that a putty–putty technology is capable of generating the same qualitative responses as a putty–clay model.

I have generalized this 'q' theory model in the previous chapter by looking at firms' decisions when they face the possibility of rationing in the goods market. The model therefore integrates the cost-minimizing approach of Abel into a more general framework, which admits a role for demand but at the same time recognizes that profitability considerations guide firms' output and investment decisions. Hence not all levels of demand will be met.

In such an integrated model we have demonstrated how firms' investment decisions depend upon the market environment. The policy problems that arise have been seen to mirror in some respects those of Malinvaud with the dependence of the appropriate policy on the regime. Equally, it has been seen that intertemporal considerations bring in additional complications. In particular, the variety of possible responses by the firm to any given change depending on initial conditions was noted. In general, without specification of the market conditions under which the firm is operating, it is impossible to give any unambiguous ranking of the speeds of adjustment of a firm to changes in demand and relative prices. This fact has important implications for model-building since, once we admit the possibility of non-market-clearing, we must recognize that the estimated coefficients obtained may be particular to certain market conditions (actual *or expected*) which no longer hold.

Notes

1. i.e., the $\dot{\mu} = 0$ locus for a firm which always produces an exogenously given level of output (in this case Q_0).
2. In fact, although the firm is definitely demand-constrained in steady state, it may be initially unconstrained. If so, the jump in μ will be smaller but still greater than for the wage rate increase; i.e., μ will jump to a point above A but possibly below B.
3. In all three cases, the instantaneous effect of an increase in wages was to produce a fall in output. The effect after this initial drop is, however, uncertain.

7

Disequilibrium Analysis and the 'q' Theory of Investment: The Case of Investment Constraints

1 Introduction

As mentioned in Chapter 4, it is now generally recognized (Abel 1979, Hayashi 1982, Yoshikawa 1980) that the neoclassical investment theory of Jorgenson modified by the assumption of adjustment costs and the theory of investment suggested by Tobin where investment is a function of 'q'—the ratio of the market value of new investment goods to their replacement cost—are equivalent. As with the earlier work of Jorgenson, 'q' theory has been based either on profit-maximizing models, where it is assumed the firm can buy and sell all the goods it wishes at the going prices, or on a cost-minimizing model of the firm, where the firm implicitly is always constrained to produce a particular level of output. A unified analysis of the firm and its investment decision where the firm may or may not face rationing has not yet been provided. In the previous chapter we considered the decisions of a firm that may face rationing in the output market. The aim of this chapter is to extend 'q' theory by considering the effects on the behaviour of the investing firms of interruptions to the desired *supply* of investment goods. The spirit of the 'q' theory literature is that 'q' tells us the incentive to invest on the part of demanding firms, but leaves the conditions under which goods are supplied very much in the background. A careful consideration of how demanding firms react when faced with constraints on their desired level of investment is therefore a necessary addition to that literature. We shall here continue the work of the previous chapters by considering the effects of investment constraints upon firms that may be both demand-constrained and unconstrained.

The discussion of delivery lags by Jorgenson and the careful analysis of the irreversibility of investment by Arrow (1968) and Nickell (1974a, 1974b) represent particular cases of constraints on the level of investment. In this chapter we seek to provide a general analysis of such constraints. The constraint therefore could be that there is a maximum rate of investment that can be done (owing to such factors as delivery lags, import controls, strikes, or capacity limitations in the capital-goods-producing industry[1]). Alternatively, the constraint could be that a minimum rate of investment must be done which could be zero and would therefore capture the idea of irreversibility. Finally, the constraints could be permanent or temporary. The analysis is therefore capable of dealing with a wide variety of cases.

As in the previous chapter, what allows a unified treatment of such cases, and allows comparison with what would have happened in the absence of the constraint, is the recognition that, as in the fix-price literature, the firm faces a new optimization problem. Different first-order conditions describe the behaviour of the firm while constrained. The trick used here is the splicing together, by means of a phase diagram, of the different sets of equations of motion implied by the different first-order conditions. The different dynamics of constrained and unconstrained cases can then be compared by inspecting the different optimal paths of the relevant variables on the phase diagram.

The plan of the chapter is as follows. In Section 2 the optimization problem of the firm is set out. In Section 3 the appropriate phase diagram is constructed for a demand constrained/cost minimizing firm, and the case of an anticipated temporary maximum to the rate of investment that can be done is examined. In Section 4, remaining with the cost-minimizing firm, various comparative-dynamic exercises are performed. In Section 5 the results are compared with those obtained for an unconstrained firm, and finally, in Section 6 the case of permanent constraints for both demand-constrained and unconstrained firms is considered.

2 Optimal Capital Accumulation with Investment Constraints

As before, the basic model is that of Abel (1979), extended by incorporating possible constraints on the level of investment the firm can undertake as in Blanchard and Sachs (1982). Purely for convenience, I present the problem only in terms of a firm that may face a maximum constraint.

Consider then, as in the previous chapters, a firm with costly adjustment of capital acting to maximize the present value of cash flows:

$$V(0) = \int_0^\infty \langle p(t)Q(t) - w(t)L(t) - [I(t) + C\{I(t)\}] \rangle e^{-rt} \, dt \quad (1)$$

where the notation is by now familiar. The firm's maximization problem is:

max (1)

subject to:
$$Q = F(K, L) \tag{2a}$$

$$Q \leqslant \bar{Q} \tag{2b}$$

$$\dot{K} = I - \delta K \tag{2c}$$

$$I \leqslant \bar{I}. \tag{2d}$$

The four constraints reflect the constraint of technology (2a), a potential demand constraint (2b), the equation of motion for the capital stock (2c), and the constraint of a maximum level of investment (2d).

Following Arrow and Kurz (1970), and following on from Chapters 4 and 5, this problem can be solved by forming the Lagrangean:

$$\mathcal{L} = [\rho F(K, L) - wL - \{I + C(I)\}] + \mu(I - \delta K)$$
$$+ \lambda_1 \{\bar{Q} - F(K, L)\} + \lambda_2 (\bar{I} - I) \tag{3}$$

where we have substituted for Q from (2a) and associated multipliers μ, λ_1, λ_2 with the constraints (2c), (2b), and (2d) respectively.

The first-order conditions for this problem are:

$$\frac{d(\mu e^{-rt})}{dt} = -\frac{\partial \mathcal{L} e^{-rt}}{\partial K}: \quad \dot{\mu} = \mu(r + \delta) - (p - \lambda_1) F_K(\cdot) \quad (4)$$

$$\frac{\partial \mathcal{L}}{\partial L} = 0: \quad (p - \lambda_1) F_L(\cdot) = w \tag{5}$$

$$\frac{\partial \mathcal{L}}{\partial I} = 0: \quad \mu - \lambda_2 = 1 + C'(I) \tag{6}$$

$$\left.\begin{array}{ll} \bar{a} \geqslant a, & \lambda_1 \geqslant 0 \\ \bar{I} \geqslant I, & \lambda_2 \geqslant 0 \end{array}\right\} \text{ with complementary slackness.} \tag{7}$$

Putting (4) and (5) together, we have
$$\dot{\mu} = \mu(r + \delta) - w \frac{F_K(\cdot)}{F_L(\cdot)} \tag{8}$$

which can be rewritten as

$$\mu(t) = \int_t^\infty w(s) \frac{F_K(s)}{F_L(s)} \exp\left\{-(r+\delta)(s-t)\right\} ds \qquad (9)$$

and says that μ is the shadow price of a unit of capital, equal, for a demand-constrained firm, to the present discounted value of wage bill savings following the installation of a unit of capital. Of course, for an unconstrained firm we know that the term $w(F_K/F_L)$ reduces to pF_K, the marginal revenue product of capital. Equation (6) says that, in the absence of any constraints on the level of investment it can undertake $(\lambda_2 = 0)$, the firm will go on investing until the marginal cost of investment, $1 + C'(I)$, is equal to the marginal benefit, μ. This is the case investigated by Abel, and we note that if $\lambda_2 = 0$ then investment is an increasing function of marginal 'q' which is here represented by μ. Thus $I = I(\mu)$ where $I'(\cdot) > 0$. When $\lambda_2 > 0$, however, and the firm is constrained in the level of investment it can undertake, we note from (7) that $I = \bar{I}$ (by definition) and from (6) that the constraint introduces a wedge between the marginal cost and benefit of investment.

3 The Demand-constrained Firm and an Anticipated Temporary Maximum Constraint on the Level of Investment

We first consider investment constraints assuming that the firm is *always* demand-constrained.[2] Assuming a constant-returns-to-scale Cobb–Douglas production function, $Q = K^\alpha L^{1-\alpha}$ where $0 < \alpha < 1$, (8) becomes

$$\dot{\mu} = \mu(r+\delta) - \frac{\alpha}{1-\alpha} w \left(\frac{\bar{Q}}{K}\right)^{1/(1-\alpha)}. \qquad (10)$$

For this cost-minimizing firm there are therefore two different cases to consider. First, where the investment constraint does not bind and so $\lambda_2 = 0, I < \bar{I}$. In this case the first-order conditions can be summarized by the equations of motion:

$$\dot{\mu} = \mu(r+\delta) - \frac{\alpha}{1-\alpha} w \left(\frac{\bar{Q}}{K}\right)^{1/(1-\alpha)} \qquad (10)$$

$$\dot{K} = I(\mu) - \delta K \qquad (11)$$

where we have simply substituted $I = I(\mu)$ (investment is an increasing function of marginal 'q') from (6) into the equation of motion for the capital stock.

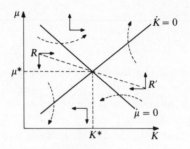

Figure 7.1

The construction of the phase diagram showing how investment and capital stock move through time is well covered in Abel (and reviewed in Chapter 5) and is therefore only briefly reviewed here. In Figure 7.1, the $\dot{\mu} = 0$ locus is drawn downward-sloping since along that locus

$$\mu(r + \delta) = \frac{\alpha}{1 - \alpha} w \left(\frac{\bar{Q}}{K} \right)^{1/(1 - \alpha)}$$

and therefore increases in K must be matched by decreases in μ to maintain the equality. Similarly, the $\dot{K} = 0$ locus is upward-sloping since along that locus $I(\mu) = \delta K$ and both $I'(\cdot)$ and $\delta > 0$. The intersection of the two stationary loci gives the steady-state position. To determine how μ and K move in the diagram, the arrows of motion are drawn. Above the $\dot{\mu} = 0$ locus,

$$\mu(r + \delta) > \frac{\alpha}{1 - \alpha} w \left(\frac{\bar{Q}}{K} \right)^{1/(1 - \alpha)}$$

and so $\dot{\mu} > 0$ and μ is rising. Conversely, below the $\dot{\mu} = 0$ locus μ is falling. Above the $\dot{K} = 0$ locus, $I(\mu) > \delta K$ and so the capital stock is growing; $\dot{K} > 0$. Conversely, below the $\dot{K} = 0$ locus, K is falling. It can be seen that the system has a saddlepoint solution with a downward-sloping stable path, RR'. At any point not on RR', the system will not converge to steady state.

We now turn to the case where the investment constraint does bind and $I = \bar{I}$. The equations of motion that now summarize the first-order conditions are:

$$\dot{\mu} = \mu(r + \delta) - \frac{\alpha}{1-\alpha} w \left(\frac{\bar{Q}}{K}\right)^{1/(1-\alpha)} \tag{10}$$

$$\dot{K} = \bar{I} - \delta K. \tag{12}$$

Thus, only the equation of motion for the capital stock is affected.[3]

In order to draw the phase diagram appropriate to the constrained investment case, we examine the stationary loci beginning with the $\dot{K} = 0$ locus. Along the $\dot{K} = 0$ locus $K = \bar{I}/\delta$. Thus there is a unique value of K, $(\bar{K})$ such that $\dot{K} = 0$, and because $\bar{I}$ is a constant, and so independent of μ, the $\dot{K} = 0$ locus is vertical. Clearly, an increase in $\bar{I}$ will shift the $\dot{K} = 0$ locus out to the right, as in Figure 7.2. To determine the behaviour of K elsewhere in the diagram, consider the $\dot{K} = 0$ locus drawn for $\bar{I} = \bar{I}_0$. To the right of the $\dot{K} = 0$ locus the required investment necessary to maintain the capital stock (δK) is greater that $\bar{I}_0$ and so K must be falling. At a point to the left of the $\dot{K} = 0$ locus $\bar{I}_0 > \delta K$ and $\dot{K} > 0$, the capital stock is growing. The arrows of motion are drawn in Figure 7.2.

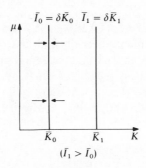

Figure 7.2

The $\dot{\mu} = 0$ locus is exactly as described in the previous case. The complete phase diagram therefore looks like Figure 7.3. The steady-state position is A, and again it can be seen that the system has a saddlepoint solution with a downward-sloping stable path SS'. From any point not on SS' the system will not reach steady state.

Finally, a reminder about a difference between the two phase diagrams. In Figure 7.1, the phase diagram describes the dynamic behaviour of μ and K, and since $I = I(\mu)$ it also tells us what is

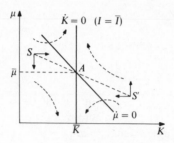

Figure 7.3

happening to investment. In Figure 7.3 the phase diagram again describes the dynamic behaviour of μ and K but, clearly, knowing μ in this case does not tell us what is happening to investment, which is fixed at $\bar{I}$. In this case μ tells us the maximum the firm would be willing to pay, taking the investment good as the numeraire, for an extra unit of capital. The discrepancy between μ and $\bar{\mu}$ defined by $1 + C'(\bar{I})$ is equal to λ_2 and so is a measure of the extent to which the constraint bites.

Suppose then that at t_0 the firm expects that, for a limited period n_0 to n_1, the maximum level of investment that can be done is $\bar{I}$. Suppose also that at t_0 the firm unexpectedly finds that demand has increased from $\bar{Q}_0$ to $\bar{Q}_1$ where the demand increase is permanent, and during the interval (n_0, n_1) the firm would like to be doing greater investment than $\bar{I}$. Ignoring the constraint on the level of investment, the response of the firm would look like Figure 7.4. The firm is initially at steady-

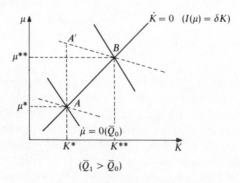

Figure 7.4

state position A. The increase in demand shifts up the $\dot{\mu} = 0$ locus. For the system to reach the new steady state, and for there to be no anticipated jumps in μ, μ must jump immediately to A' on the new stable path and move down $A'B$ thereafter.

The time path of investment and the capital stock look like Figure 7.5. I^* is the initial steady-state level of investment. Following the unanticipated increase in demand, investment jumps to $I(t_0)$, corresponding to point A' in Figure 7.4 and gradually declining to the new steady-state level of investment I^{**} as the firm moves along the stable path $A'B$. The capital stock increases, though at a diminishing rate, to K^{**}. Assuming for convenience that $\bar{I} = I^{**}$, the final steady-state level of investment, how should the firm react to this anticipated constraint? Clearly, several possibilities exist.

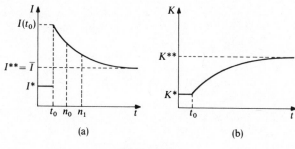

Figure 7.5

1. The firm could do nothing, carrying on with exactly the same investment policy until n_0, when it would be constrained to carry out only investment $\bar{I}$; after n_1, because it would now have a smaller capital stock than on the unconstrained path, the firm could carry out more investment. In other words, all adjustment to the constraint would come after n_1.

2. The firm could decide to do sufficient extra investment before n_0 that at n_1 it had exactly the same capital stock as if unconstrained, and so pursued the same investment policy after n_1. In this case all adjustment to the constraint comes before n_1.

3. Finally, the firm could spread the effects of the constraint both before n_0 and after n_1 by doing more investment both before and after the constraint interval.

Formally, the problem is to construct a path for (μ, K) that satisfies the equations of motion (10), (11) for $t_0 < t < n_0$ and $t \geq n_1$ and the equations of motion (10), (12) for $n_0 \leqslant t < n_1$. This requires the combination of Figures 7.1 and 7.3.

The complete phase diagram is drawn in Figure 7.6. By assumption, the constrained level of investment $\bar{I}$ is equal to the steady-state level of investment I^{**} which is just sufficient to maintain the final steady-state capital stock K^{**}. The constrained $\dot{K} = 0$ locus is located therefore by drawing a vertical line through capital stock K^{**} as described in Section 2. Although the steady-state position is the same for both constrained and unconstrained cases, it is shown in Appendix B to this chapter that the stable path corresponding to the constrained steady state is steeper than the stable path for the unconstrained steady state.

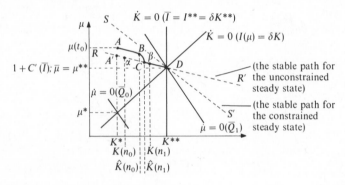

Figure 7.6

The precise path followed by μ, K in the phase diagram is governed by several requirements. First of all, the path of μ must be continuous, as was discussed earlier in Chapter 3. Second, for $t_0 < t < n_0$ (μ, K) are driven by (10), (11). During this interval the initial jump and subsequent movement of μ is governed by the condition that at n_1 we must be back on the stable path RR' in order to reach the final steady state with no jumps in μ. Thus μ must jump initially to give a continuous path for μ, K when driven by (10), (11) for $t_0 < t < n_0$ and (10), (12) for $n_0 \leqslant t < n_1$ which just hits the stable path RR' at n_1. *ABCD* is such a path.

Note immediately that the initial jump in μ $(\mu(t_0))$ is larger than would otherwise have occurred. This has to be the case. Suppose instead that μ had jumped only to A', as in the unconstrained case. Then during the interval $(t_0 - n_0)\mu$, K would, because driven by (10), (11), have moved down the stable path RR'. During the interval $(n_0 - n_1)$, however, (μ, K) are driven by equations of motion (11), (12). By definition (μ, K) cannot continue to move along RR' when driven by (11), (12). If it were true it would imply that, if the investment constraint held indefinitely, the system would reach steady state. But we know that the stable path corresponding to the constrained system, which is the only path leading to steady state for the constrained system, lies above RR' for $K < K^{**}$. Since SS' is steeper than RR', and since RR' lies below SS', (μ, K) will follow a steeper path than along RR' during this period. Therefore at n_1, μ would lie below the stable path and μ must jump in order to reach RR' and steady-state D. This discontinuity is inconsistent with a unique path along which expectations are fulfilled, and this path can therefore be ruled out. *A fortiori*, so can an initial jump in μ that would put the firm below RR'. Thus μ must jump initially above RR', and so over the period $(t_0 - n_0)$ the firm is doing more investment than otherwise.

Along the optimal path $ABCD$, the length of time taken to traverse AB is $t_0 - n_0$. μ, K are driven by (10), (11) during this interval. At n_0 the firm is at point B in the phase diagram compared with the point α, where the firm would be at n_0 if unconstrained. Clearly, at B the firm has a higher capital stock than at α, reflecting the higher rate of investment over $(t_0 - n_0)$; μ, it will also be noted, is higher, reflecting the imminent constraint on the level of investment, implying lower future capital stocks and therefore higher marginal products and so a higher value of μ. Over BC the firm is governed by (10), (12), and the length of time taken to traverse BC is $(n_0 - n_1)$. At n_1 (μ, K) just hits RR' with no anticipatable jumps in μ as required.

The phase diagram can therefore be used to rule out one of the possibilities discussed earlier. Option 1 is clearly wrong, since the firm does react to the anticipated constraint by doing more investment initially. However, it is not possible simply by inspection of the phase diagram to choose between the remaining possibilities. How much more investment does the firm do initially? Is it such that at n_1 the firm has exactly the same capital stock as when unconstrained? Or is it smaller, in which case the constrained firm will be doing more investment than the unconstrained firm after n_1 as well?

To rule out this latter possibility, consider the following simple proof. Suppose that it were true, and that the firm therefore has the same capital stock at n_1 as in the unconstrained case. Let

$\mu(t)$ = the value of μ at time t for the unconstrained firm;

$\hat{\mu}(t)$ = the value of μ at time t for the constrained firm;

$K(t)$, $\hat{K}(t)$ = the capital stock at time t of the unconstrained and constrained firms, respectively;

$I(t)$, $\hat{I}(t)$ = the investment rates at t of the constrained and unconstrained firms, respectively.

By definition,

$$
\begin{aligned}
\mu(t_0) &= \int_{t_0}^{\infty} \frac{\alpha}{1-\alpha} w \left\{ \frac{\bar{Q}_1}{K(s)} \right\}^{1/(1-\alpha)} \exp\{-(r+\delta)(s-t_0)\}\, ds \\
&= \int_{t_0}^{n_1} \frac{\alpha}{1-\alpha} w \left\{ \frac{\bar{Q}_1}{K(s)} \right\}^{1/(1-\alpha)} \exp\{-(r+\delta)(s-t_0)\}\, ds \\
&\quad + \int_{n_1}^{\infty} \frac{\alpha}{1-\alpha} w \left\{ \frac{Q_1}{K(s)} \right\}^{1/(1-\alpha)} \exp\{-(r+\delta)(s-t_0)\}\, ds.
\end{aligned}
$$

Similarly,

$$
\begin{aligned}
\hat{\mu}(t_0) &= \int_{t_0}^{n_1} \frac{\alpha}{1-\alpha} w \left\{ \frac{\bar{Q}_1}{\hat{K}(s)} \right\}^{1/(1-\alpha)} \exp\{-(r+\delta)(s-t_0)\}\, ds \\
&\quad + \int_{n_1}^{\infty} \frac{\alpha}{1-\alpha} w \left\{ \frac{\bar{Q}_1}{\hat{K}(s)} \right\}^{1/(1-\alpha)} \exp\{-(r+\delta)(s-t_0)\}\, ds.
\end{aligned}
$$

Since $K(t) = \hat{K}(t)\ \forall\, t \geqslant n_1$ by hypothesis, then

$$
\begin{aligned}
\mu(t_0) - \hat{\mu}(t_0) &= \int_{t_0}^{n_1} \frac{\alpha}{1-\alpha} w \left\{ \frac{\bar{Q}_1}{K(s)} \right\}^{1/(1-\alpha)} \exp\{-(r+\delta)(s-t_0)\}\, ds \\
&\quad - \int_{t_0}^{n_1} \frac{\alpha}{1-\alpha} w \left\{ \frac{\bar{Q}_1}{\hat{K}(s)} \right\}^{1/(1-\alpha)} \\
&\qquad \times \exp\{-(r+\delta)(s-t_0)\}\, ds.
\end{aligned}
$$

Again, by hypothesis, $\hat{I}(t) > I(t)$ for $t_0 \leqslant t < n_0$ and $\bar{I} < I(t)$ for $n_0 \leqslant t < n_1$; that is, since the constrained firm does more investment $(t_0 - n_0)$ and then less investment $(n_0 - n_1)$, and has the same capital stock at n_1 as the unconstrained, then it must be true that $\hat{K}(t) > K(t)$ for all $t_0 < t < n_1$.

But then

$$\frac{\bar{Q}_1}{K(t)} > \frac{\bar{Q}_1}{\hat{K}(t)} \ \forall \, t_0 < t < n_1$$

and therefore $\mu(t_0) - \hat{\mu}(t_0) > 0$.

But this is a contradiction, since $\hat{\mu}(t_0) < \mu(t_0)$ implies that $\hat{I}(t_0) < I(t_0)$. *A fortiori*, the same argument rules out the firm having a larger capital stock at n_1 when having been constrained. Thus at n_1, $\hat{K}(n_1) < K(n_1)$, the firm is 'higher up' the stable path RR' (point C as opposed to point β) and so is doing more investment than otherwise. Thus the path of investment along $ABCD$ looks like Figure 7.7, where the constrained investment path is represented by *abcdef* and the unconstrained investment path by $a_0b_0e_0f$.

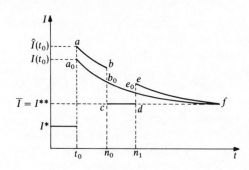

Figure 7.7

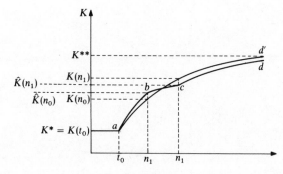

Figure 7.8

The firm, then, does indeed react to an anticipated constraint by 'spreading' the effects of that constraint. More investment than on the unconstrained path is done both before and after the period of constraint, and the constrained firm has a larger capital stock at the beginning of the constraint interval ($\hat{K}(n_0) > K(n_0)$) but a smaller capital stock at the end of the interval ($\hat{K}(n_1) < K(n_1)$). This is all illustrated in Figure 7.6. The path of the capital stock looks like Figure 7.8, where *abcd* represents the path of capital stock of an constrained firm and *ad'* the path of capital stock of an unconstrained firm.

4 Some Comparative Dynamic Exercises

(a) *The Effect of Increasing the Length of the Constraint Period*

Suppose now the firm expects that the interval over which it can do only investment $\bar{I}$ to increase from $(n_0 - n_1)$ to $(n_0 - n_2)$. Consider the phase diagram in Figure 7.6. The length of time taken to travel along AB is $t_0 - n_0$ and along BC, $n_0 - n_1$. Clearly, then, this path is no longer optimal since the period of constraint is now greater, and so if the path ABC were followed we would be at a point below the stable path RR' at n_2 rather than just on it, as required. In other words, the time taken to traverse BC is too short, and we must have a path such as $A'B'C'$ in Figure 7.9 if we are simultaneously to satisfy the requirements that the time spent over the constrained portion of the path be longer and that there be no anticipated jumps in μ. The time path of

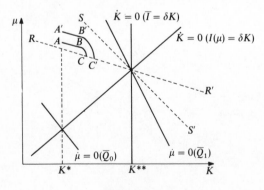

Figure 7.9

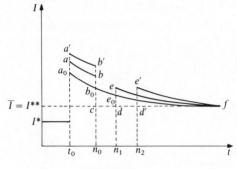

Figure 7.10

investment looks like Figure 7.10, where $a_0 b_0 e_0 f$ represents the unconstrained investment path, $abcdef$ the investment path for constraint period $(n_0 - n_1)$, and $a'b'cd'e'f$ the investment path for constraint period $(n_0 - n_2)$.

Thus, the firm reacts to an anticipated lengthening of the period of constraint by doing more investment than otherwise both before and after.[4] So $a'b'$ lies everywhere above ab and $e'f$ lies everywhere above the path ef for all $t \geqslant n$. This is an expected result, since the firm is in a sense clearly 'more constrained' when the constraint period is longer and we would therefore expect 'more' of the result that we got in Section 3.

(b) Increasing the Severity of the Constraint

Assume now that the constraint period is $n_0 - n_1$ but that during this interval the firm can carry out an investment of only $\bar{\bar{I}} < \bar{I}$. The effect of this is to shift the relevant $\dot{K} = 0$ locus to the left, and the new constrained stable path is TT'. The phase diagram with the new optimal path $A'B'C'$ is shown in Figure 7.11. Because the equation of motion for K has changed to $\dot{K} = \bar{\bar{I}} - \delta K$ over the interval $(n_0 - n_1)$, the path ABC is no longer optimal. Suppose though that the firm had followed the path AB and had done exactly the same amount of investment as prior to the constraint interval, and so at n_0 is at point B. From $n_0 - n_1$, however, the firm is no longer doing investment $\bar{I}$ but $\bar{\bar{I}}$, and so the growth in the capital stock will be smaller. The firm will be at a point to the left of point C in the diagram and *below the stable path* RR'. To see this more fully, consider the arrows of motion operating

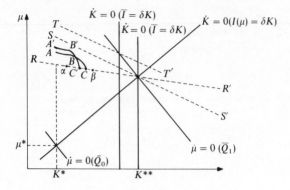

Figure 7.11

at B with constraints $\bar{I}$ and $\bar{\bar{I}}$, respectively. Because the $\dot{\mu} = 0$ locus is unaffected, the downward pull on μ represented by the vertical arrow of motion is the same in both cases. However, as I have argued, the rate of increase of K is now smaller, as represented by the horizontal arrow of motion. Thus the paths of (μ, K) in the two cases look like Figure 7.12. Over the same interval $(n_0 - n_1)$, then, K must increase less and μ fall by more. Thus we must begin the constrained phase at a point above B which requires greater investment prior to n_0 as along $A'B'$. Finally, by using the same algebraic proof as in Section 2, we can rule out the firm having the same or larger capital stock at n_1 with the constraint $\bar{\bar{I}}$ as the firm facing constraint $\bar{I}$. Thus $B'C'$ must cut BC so that the firm has a lower capital stock at n_1.

Case 1: $I = \bar{I}$ Case 2: $I = \bar{\bar{I}}$

Figure 7.12

The full paths of investment and capital stock therefore look like Figure 7.13, where the investment path of an unconstrained firm is represented by $a_0 b_0 e_0 f$; the investment path of a firm constrained to do investment $\bar{I}$ over $n_0 - n_1$ by $abcdef$; the investment path of a firm constrained to do investment $\bar{\bar{I}}$ over $n_0 - n_1$ by $a'b'c'd'e'f$; the

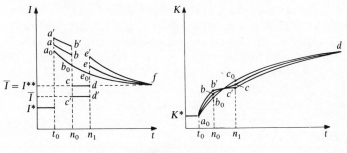

Figure 7.13

unconstrained firm's capital stock by $a_0 b_0 c_0 d$; the $\bar{I}$-constrained firm by $a_0 bcd$; and the $\bar{\bar{I}}$-constrained firm by $a_0 b'c'd$.

(c) Minimum Constraints

Without going through the full analysis, it should be clear that the same general conclusions carry over for the case of a minimum constraint where the firm is constrained to do investment $\bar{I}$ during an interval but would like to do less. Thus for $t_0 \leqslant t < n_0$ the firm will do less investment than otherwise, and similarly after n_1. Also, the steeper the constraint, either because of a longer constraint period or an increase in $\bar{I}$, the more the firm will react by doing less investment both before and after the period of constraint.

5 Investment Constraints and the Unconstrained Firm

We now turn to the effects of investment constraints upon the unconstrained firm. Thus far we have seen how, in line with intuition, the demand-constrained firm reacts to an anticipated investment constraint by trying to spread the effects of the constraint. For a maximum constraint, the lower investment over the constrained period reduces the firm's anticipated capital stock and so raises anticipated marginal products, 'q', and hence current investment. Investment is also higher than otherwise when the constraint is lifted. We shall see in this section that these conclusions do not hold for the unconstrained firm. For a constant-returns-to-scale profit-maximizing firm, as we saw in Chapter 5, the marginal product of both capital and labour is determined entirely by the real wage and depends only upon the capital–labour *ratio*. As is well known, what makes the scale of operations determinate for such a firm is the assumption of adjustment costs that determine the optimal rate of investment, which in turn determines the firm's capital stock. Given this, interruptions to the time path of the capital stock caused by investment constraints will therefore be met by adjustments to output and employment, leaving the capital–labour ratio and hence μ unchanged. The firm does not therefore react at all to an anticipated temporary constraint.

To illustrate this, we again consider the case of an anticipated temporary maximum constraint on the level of investment. For the firm that is not demand-constrained, the first-order conditions for the case where the investment constraint does not bite can be summarized, as in Chapter 5, by the equations of motion:

$$\dot{\mu} = \mu(r+\delta) - p\alpha\left(\frac{1}{1-\alpha}\frac{w}{p}\right)^{(\alpha-1)/\alpha}$$

$$\dot{K} = I(\mu) - \delta K.$$

The phase diagram for this case is familar and therefore will not be not repeated here. When the investment constraint does bind, the equations of motion naturally become

$$\dot{\mu} = \mu(r+\delta) - p\alpha\left(\frac{1}{1-\alpha}\frac{w}{p}\right)^{(\alpha-1)/\alpha}$$

$$\dot{K} = \bar{I} - \delta K.$$

Integrating forward the equation of motion for μ to give

$$\mu(t) = \int_t^\infty p\alpha\left(\frac{1}{1-\alpha}\frac{w}{p}\right)^{(\alpha-1)/\alpha} \exp\{-(r+\delta)(s-t)\}\,ds$$

makes plain that the value of μ is entirely unaffected by the constraint on the level of investment $\bar{I}$. It is straightforward to verify this by drawing the phase diagram corresponding to the constrained case, the details of which should be obvious given earlier discussion.

In Figure 7.14 we can see that, although there is a given level of investment, $\bar{I}$, the stable path is still the $\dot{\mu} = 0$ locus, reflecting the fact that it is the capital–labour ratio that determines μ rather than the size of the capital stock *per se*. But this means immediately that, in the face of an anticipated temporary constraint as in Section 4, the only

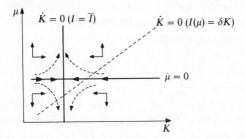

Figure 7.14

continuous path for μ is that which leaves it on the $\dot{\mu} = 0$ locus. Hence μ and current investment are unaffected by the anticipated constraint. The firm pursues exactly the same investment, output, and employment policies both before and after the constraint. During the constrained period, however, investment, output, and employment are all lower as the optimal capital–labour ratio is maintained.

By the same arguments, increasing the length of the constraint period and the severity of the constraint also has no effects upon investment levels before the period of constraint. A more severe constraint however will reduce output and employment further during the constraint period as the capital stock is further reduced compared with what it would have been. Finally, as before, these arguments hold equally for minimum constraints.

6 Permanent Constraints and Irreversibility

We now consider permanent constraints on the level of investment the firm can undertake either as a maximum ($I \leqslant I \max \forall t$) or as a minimum ($I \geqslant I \min \forall t$). Clearly, one possibility included within this general analysis is

$$I \min = 0 \quad \forall t,$$

which covers the case of irreversibility studied by Arrow and Nickell.

As before, we begin with the case of the demand-constrained firm and state a general conclusion of which Section 4 is suggestive but which has not yet been proved:

If ever such a firm encounters a maximum constraint on the amount of investment it can do, then, *ceteris paribus*, this must raise the value of marginal 'q' (μ) above what it would otherwise be.

Proof. Consider the firm during a constrained investment phase where the constraint could be temporary or permanent. The value of μ is given by (on our assumptions)

$$\mu(t) = \int_t^\infty \frac{\alpha}{1-\alpha}\, w \left\{ \frac{\bar{Q}}{\hat{K}(s)} \right\}^{1/(1-\alpha)} \exp \left\{ -(r+\delta)(s-t) \right\} ds.$$

Now suppose the constraint is unexpectedly lifted. By definition, the firm must expect its capital stock to be larger than it would otherwise be for at least some future t and no greater for all other t. Hence $Q/K(\cdot)$ must be smaller than otherwise for at least some future t and no greater for all other t. Thus μ must fall. But this says that for any given K, while the firm is constrained, the value of μ must be higher than it would be if that firm faced no investment constraint: otherwise an unexpected lifting of the constraint would not lead to a fall in μ. If on the other hand the constraint lies in the future, again either becuase of a temporary constraint that is anticipated or because of the existence of a permanent constraint which the firm knows will be binding, then clearly μ, and therefore investment, must increase currently above what it would otherwise be if an anticipated jump in μ is to be avoided.

Given the above, two cases in which a permanent constraint bites are straightforward: (1) where a maximum exists which the firm expects to hit and then remain constrained thereafter; (2) where a maximum exists and an unanticipated change takes place which cause the firm to become unavoidably constrained (see Figure 7.15). In the first case the firm will clearly do more investment in advance of the constraint and may even hit the constraint immediately. In the second case the firm will simply invest $\bar{I}$ until such time as it has a sufficiently large capital stock to become unconstrained.

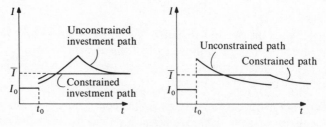

Figure 7.15

The interesting case is where, although a permanent maximum constraint exists, the firm expects to become constrained but also later expects to become unconstrained. Suppose then the firm receives news at t_0 which causes the desired investment path to move along *abc* in Figure 7.16. However, $\bar{I}$ is the maximum level of investment that can be done. The full phase diagram for this case is drawn in Appendix C at the end of this chapter. Without knowing the precise path to be followed, we can nevertheless, using our earlier discussion, analyse this case quite straightforwardly. First, μ must rise at t_0 above what it would otherwise do since the firm encounters a maximum investment constraint. Investment therefore also rises at t_0. This causes the firm to hit the constraint sooner than otherwise (at time $\hat{t}$). Second, for all $t_0 < t \leqslant t'$ the firm facing the constraint does more investment, while for $t' < t < t''$ it does less than the unconstrained firm. This raises the possibility that at t'' the constrained firm has the same capital stock as the unconstrained firm and would therefore pursue the same investment path *cd* where $I \ll \bar{I}$. Again, this possibility can be ruled out by the usual algebraic proof given in Section 3. The optimal path for investment of the firm facing a permanent constraint $\bar{I}$ must then be one such as $a'b'c'd'$. As in Section 4, the demand-constrained firm reacts to the anticipated constraint by spreading the effects—doing more investment in anticipation of the constraint and more investment after t''.

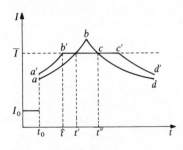

Figure 7.16

Again, as in Section 4, although we have examined maximum constraints, the same general conclusions can be applied to minimum constraints; in particular, we have the same conclusion for the particular case of irreversibility where $I \geqslant \bar{I} = 0$ as does Nickell—the firm anticipating the irreversibility constraint, and so being left with capital stock it would otherwise dispose of, reacts to this by investing less both before and after it would otherwise become constrained.

Turning to the non-demand-constrained firm, the conclusions of Section 5 carry over. Because μ is determined by the capital–labour ratio, which in turn is determined by the real wage, a constraint on the level of investment that the firm can carry out does not alter the value of μ, and hence the investment path of the firm is unaffected by any anticipation of a constraint, either permanent or temporary.

7 Conclusion

This chapter has provided a general analysis of investment constraints in a neoclassical model. The model is, as in earlier chapters, of both a cost-minimizing (demand-constrained) and a profit-maximizing firm with a putty–putty technology and subject to strictly convex costs of adjustment. Since such a neoclassical model so amended is equivalent to Tobin's 'q' theory, this chapter provides an extension of 'q' theory to take account of investment constraints. We have seen that formally irreversibility, studied by Nickell and Arrow, is a particular instance of the general problem of investment constraints, and the results of irreversibility follow naturally from an analysis of the more general problem.

The results obtained differ according to whether the firm is demand-constrained or not. For the demand-constrained firm the profitability of a unit of capital depends upon the size of the capital stock, and hence maximum constraints on the level of investment of the firm raise the value of marginal 'q' by making the future capital stock of the firm lower than otherwise. Where such a constraint can be anticipated, this leads to the firm increasing investment before the constraint is hit. By contrast, for an unconstrained firm marginal 'q' is completely unaltered by an investment constraint, since marginal 'q' depends only upon the capital–labour ratio and the firm reacts to an investment constraint only when it occurs by reducing employment and output.

Appendix A Proof that the Equation of Motion for μ is Unaltered by an Investment Constraint

In general, the capital stock at any time t is given by

$$K(t) = \int_{-\infty}^{t} I(s)\exp\{-\delta(t-s)\}\,ds. \tag{i}$$

But during a constrained investment path we can be more precise. Assuming that the period of constraint began at n_0 and that the firm is still constrained at t, then

$$K(t) = \int_{-\infty}^{n_0} I(s) \exp\{-\delta(t-s)\} ds + \int_{n_0}^{t} \bar{I} \exp\{-\delta(t-s)\} ds$$

$$= \exp\{-\delta(t-n_0)\} K(n_0) + \frac{\bar{I}}{\delta} \int_{n_0}^{t} \exp\{-\delta(t-s)\} ds. \qquad \text{(ii)}$$

$$\therefore \; K(t) = \exp\{-\delta(t-n_0)\} K(n_0) + \frac{\bar{I}}{\delta} [1 - \exp\{-\delta(t-n_0)\}].$$

$$\text{(iii)}$$

The definition of μ is

$$\mu(t) = \int_{t}^{\infty} \frac{\alpha}{1-\alpha} w \left\{ \frac{\bar{Q}}{K(s)} \right\}^{1/(1-\alpha)} \exp\{-(r+\delta)(s-t)\} ds$$

where differentiation with respect to t yields (10). But this fails to take account of the fact that we know more about the path of $K(\cdot)$ along a constrained investment path, and therefore it might seem that the equation of motion for μ could be different. Thus, we should take explicit account of the behaviour of $K(\cdot)$ over a constrained period (n_0, n_1) and then derive the equation of motion for μ.

Consider then the value of μ during a constrained investment period $n_0 < t < n_1$:

$$\mu(t) = \int_{t}^{n_1} \frac{\alpha}{1-\alpha} w \left\{ \frac{\bar{Q}}{K(s)} \right\}^{1/(1-\alpha)} \exp\{-(r+\delta)(s-t)\} ds$$

$$+ \int_{n_1}^{\infty} \frac{\alpha}{1-\alpha} w \left\{ \frac{\bar{Q}}{K(s)} \right\}^{1/(1-\alpha)} \exp\{-(r+\delta)(s-t)\} ds$$

$$= \int_{t}^{n_1} \frac{\alpha}{1-\alpha} w \left\{ \frac{\bar{Q}}{K(s)} \right\}^{1/(1-\alpha)} \exp\{-(r+\delta)(s-t)\} ds$$

$$+ \exp\{-(r+\delta)(n_1-t)\} \mu(n_1). \qquad \text{(iv)}$$

But during a constrained interval, from (iii),

$$K(s) = \exp\{-\delta(s-t)\} K(t) + \frac{\bar{I}}{\delta} [1 - \exp\{-\delta(s-t)\}]. \qquad \text{(v)}$$

Substituting (v) into (iv),

$$\mu(t) = \int_{t}^{n_1} \frac{\alpha}{1-\alpha}\, w \bar{Q}^{1/(1-\alpha)} \left\langle K(t) \exp\{-\delta(s-t)\} \right.$$

$$\left. + \frac{\bar{I}}{\delta}[1 - \exp\{-\delta(s-t)\}] \right\rangle^{-1/(1-\alpha)}$$

$$\times \exp\{-(r+\delta)(s-t)\}\, ds + \exp\{-(r+\delta)(n_1 - t)\}\, \mu(n_1). \qquad \text{(vi)}$$

Differentiating this expression with respect to t still, however, gives (10). Thus the equation of motion for μ is indeed unaffected on a constrained investment path, because the constraint is a restriction not on $K(\cdot)$ itself (or on $Q(\cdot)$ or $L(\cdot)$), but rather on the rate of change of $K(\cdot)$.

Appendix B   Proof that the Stable Path of the Constrained Investment Equilibrium is Steeper than the Stable Arm of the Unconstrained Equilibrium When They Lead to the Same Steady State

Consider a point such as α on the unconstrained stable path in Figure A7.1. At α, $\dot{\mu}$ is the same for both the constrained and the unconstrained cases since the $\dot{\mu} = 0$ locus is the same for both cases.

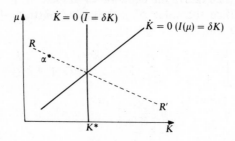

Figure A7.1

However, for the unconstrained case, $\dot{K} = I(\mu) - \delta K$, which is greater than for the constrained case, where $\dot{K} = \bar{I} - \delta K$ since $I(\mu) > \bar{I}$. Therefore the arrows of motion at α look like Figure A7.2.

Thus, a point such as α on RR', when governed by the constrained equations of motion, will not lead to the steady-state position, and the

Constrained case   Unconstrained case

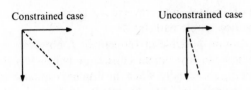

Figure A7.2

constrained stable path must lie above the unconstrained stable path for all $K < K^*$ and so is steeper.

Appendix C   The Phase Diagram for the Case of Permanent Constraints and the Demand-constrained Firm (applicable to irreversibility)

In Figure A7.3, consider at t_0 news of a permanent increase in demand from $\bar{Q}_0$ to $\bar{Q}_1$ at time t_1, which would lead to investment path ABC. The equations of motion for the unconstrained case are:

$$t_0 \leqslant t < t_1 \quad \left.\begin{array}{l} \dot{\mu} = \mu(r+\delta) - \dfrac{\alpha}{1-\alpha} w \left(\dfrac{\bar{Q}_0}{K}\right)^{1/(1-\alpha)} \\[2ex] \dot{K} = I(\mu) - \delta K \end{array}\right\} \tag{i}$$

$$t \geqslant t_1 \quad \left.\begin{array}{l} \dot{\mu} = \mu(r+\delta) - \dfrac{\alpha}{1-\alpha} w \left(\dfrac{\bar{Q}_1}{K}\right)^{1/(1-\alpha)} \\[2ex] \dot{K} = I(\mu) - \delta K. \end{array}\right\} \tag{ii}$$

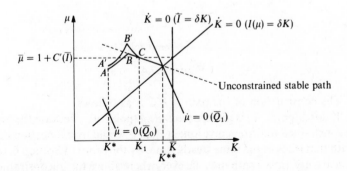

Figure A7.3

The length of time taken to traverse AB is $t_1 - t_0$ so that the system just hits the new stable path (at B) at t_1.

With maximum possible investment of $\bar{I}$, however, the firm will clearly run into an investment constraint (when $\mu > \bar{\mu}$) and must anticipate doing so. Equally, when the firm has capital stock K_1 it will become unconstrained. Four different sets of equations of motion are therefore relevant for this problem:

1. $t_0 \leqslant t$ and until the firm becomes constrained: as (i) above;
2. after the firm first becomes constrained until t_1:

$$\left.\begin{aligned}\dot{\mu} &= \mu(r+\delta) - \frac{\alpha}{1-\alpha} w\left(\frac{\bar{Q}_0}{K}\right)^{1/(1-\alpha)} \\ \dot{K} &= \bar{I} - \delta K\end{aligned}\right\} \tag{i$'$}$$

3. $t_1 \leqslant t$ and until the firm becomes unconstrained:

$$\left.\begin{aligned}\dot{\mu} &= \mu(r+\delta) - \frac{\alpha}{1-\alpha} w\left(\frac{\bar{Q}_1}{K}\right)^{1/(1-\alpha)} \\ \dot{K} &= \bar{I} - \delta K\end{aligned}\right\} \tag{ii$'$}$$

4. for all t after the firm becomes unconstrained: as (ii) above.

An optimal path for (μ, K) in this case is one such as $A'B'C$. Expanding this part of the diagram to give more detail, it looks like Figure A7.4.

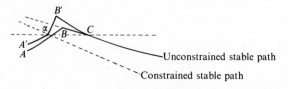

Figure A7.4

The construction of the path $A'B'C$ is as follows.

1. $\hat{\mu}(t_0)$ (point A') is greater than $\mu(t_0)$ (point A)—because the firm is constrained to do less investment than it would over a portion of a path that leads to the same steady state. By the proof of Section 6, the constrained (μ, K) path must lie everywhere above the unconstrained path (since if the constraint were unexpectedly lifted μ must fall).

2. The firm therefore does more investment and hits the constraint sooner and is governed by the behaviour of (μ, K) equations of motion (i) until the constraint is hit, at α.

3. At α there is a discrete change in the slope of the μ, K path (which becomes steeper), since $\dot{K}^{\text{CD}} < \dot{K}^{\text{UCD}}$ since $\bar{I} < I(\mu)$. The arrows of motion change from

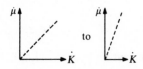

At t_1 the firm must be at a point B' above the newly relevant unconstrained path—since, again, if the constraint is unexpectedly lifted then *ceteris paribus* μ must fall. The path of μ, K is now governed by equations of motion (ii') and must be such as to hit the new unconstrained stable path at C with no jumps in μ.

4. Along CD the behaviour of μ, K is governed by equations of motion (ii). The path of investment of the constrained and unconstrained firm is therefore as depicted in Figure 7.16.

Notes

1. We shall take a closer look at this particular question in Chapter 8.
2. To introduce at this stage the possibility of regime-switching as in Chapter 5 would unnecessarily complicate the discussion.
3. Given the pattern of the earlier chapters, this result may seem slightly strange. For a proof of this, therefore, see Appendix A at the end of this chapter.
4. It has not been proved that the firm will be doing more investment at n_2 than in the previous two cases considered (unconstrained and constraint period of $(n_0 - n_1)$). To do so would simply require a repetition of the algebraic proof in Section 3.

8

Investment, Time, and Capacity Constraints

1 Introduction

In Chapters 5 and 6 we have looked at the implications of generalizing neoclassical 'q' theory to take account of non-market-clearing in the product market. While the different market conditions faced by demanding firms affected 'q', it remained true that investment behaviour was demand-determined. This was implied by relating investment to marginal 'q' where marginal 'q' is defined as the ratio of demand price to the market price of new capital goods. Given this definition, what then determines the particular investment path chosen and the divergence of market value from replacement cost is the specification of adjustment costs, $C(I)$, broadly intended to capture the notion that more rapid adjustment is costly.

All this ignores any attention to the behaviour of the capital-goods-producing industry and essentially assumes two things about the supply side of the market: first, that the incentive is always there to produce new capital goods, and second, that, even if there is such an incentive, the goods can become available instantaneously. If either of these assumptions does not hold, then, as we shall see, investment may not be a function of 'q' as defined above and the usual specification of adjustment costs may not account for the behaviour of marginal 'q'. In Chapters 3 and 7 some elements of supply-side behaviour have been considered. Chapter 3 looked at the implications for aggregate investment of the specification of an upward-sloping industry supply function where increases in capital goods prices were necessary to call forth additional supply. Nevertheless, the specification of the immediate reaction of investment to capital goods prices does assume that production of investment goods can respond instantaneously. In Chapter 7 we turned to the question of how interruptions to supply can be incorporated into 'q' theory. While an immediate implication is that, during the period of constraint, investment is supply-determined and no longer a function of 'q', the focus was on how the anticipation of the constraint affected the behaviour of demanding firms. The constraints considered were exogenous and so were beyond the influence of demanding firms, while, in contrast to Chapter 3, the analysis assumed that capital goods prices were given.

This chapter again looks at the supply side of the investment goods market where we make particular assumptions about behaviour in order to incorporate the above considerations: in response to an increase in demand, new investment goods are not instantaneously available and time must elapse before new capacity can be built and supply increased. Although supply-side behaviour is not derived from an optimizing model, the particular specification used is quite common and serves to illustrate what can happen when supply considerations are introduced. What the analysis shows is how, if one tries, by specifying what happens to supply as demand is increased, to look at the actual costs that might be involved, either in the form of delays in the availability of capital or in the form of increases in the price of capital goods, the relationship between investment, 'q', and capital goods prices might be quite different from that suggested by conventional 'q' theory associated with the very general assumption of adjustment costs.

2 The Model

(a) The Demand Side of the Market

In order to address the question of the behaviour of firms faced with potential delays in the availability of capital, we first look at the optimal accumulation policy of a firm that is subject to supply-side constraints. This has already been done in the previous chapter, and so we know the firm's maximization problem can be written

$$\max V(0) = \int_0^\infty \{F(K, L) - wL - p_1 C(I)\} e^{-rt} dt \tag{1}$$

subject to $\dot{K} = I - \delta K$ (2a)

$I \leqslant I^s$ where I^s is investment supply (2b)

$Q \leqslant \bar{Q}.$ (2c)

This formulation is slightly changed from that of the previous chapter. The price of capital goods has been made explicit, and a slightly different specification of the adjustment cost function has been used because this simplifies examination of the role of capital goods prices in determining marginal 'q'. We adopt the usual assumption that actual investment is determined by the short side of the market: $I = \min(I^d, I^s)$. The Hamiltonian for this problem is

$$H = \{F(K, L) - wL - p_I C(I)\} + \mu(I - \delta K) + \lambda_1 (I^s - I)$$
$$+ \lambda_2 \{\bar{Q} - F(K, L)\} \tag{3}$$

with first-order conditions

$$\dot{\mu} = \mu(r + \delta) - (1 - \lambda_2) F_K(\cdot) \tag{4}$$

$$(1 - \lambda_2) F_L(\cdot) = w \tag{5}$$

$$(\mu - \lambda_1) = p_I C'(I) \tag{6}$$

$$\lambda_1 (I^s - I), \ \lambda_2 (\bar{Q} - Q) = 0. \tag{7}$$

In this section we will concentrate on the case of the demand-constrained/cost-minimizing firm (i.e., $\lambda_2 > 0$). If such a firm can carry out its desired investment plans ($\lambda_1 = 0$), then the first-order conditions become

$$C'(I) = \frac{\mu(t)}{p_I(t)}$$

$$= \int_0^\infty w(s) \frac{F_K(s)}{F_L(s)} \exp\{-(r + \delta)(s - t)\} \, ds \bigg/ p_I(t) \tag{8}$$

and therefore

$$I = I^d = I(q) \text{ where } \partial I/\partial q > 0 \text{ and } q = \mu/p_I$$
$$= \text{marginal } 'q'.$$

The equation of motion for 'q', obtained simply from differentiation of (8), is therefore

$$\dot{q} = q\left(r + \delta - \frac{\dot{p}_I}{p_I}\right) - \frac{w}{p_I} \frac{F_K(\cdot)}{F_L(\cdot)} \tag{9}$$

which becomes

$$\dot{q} = q(r + \delta) - \frac{wF_K(\cdot)}{\bar{p}_I F_L(\cdot)},$$

as previously, if the price of capital goods is unchanging at $\bar{p}_I$. For the firm that is unconstrained in the product market, (9) reduces to

$$\dot{q} = q\left(r + \delta - \frac{\dot{p}_I}{\bar{p}_I}\right) - \frac{F_K(\cdot)}{p_I}. \tag{10}$$

(b) *The Supply Side of the Market*

For producers of new capital goods, we have chosen to assume the simple supply curve of Figure 8.1, which nevertheless enjoys some popularity and is a special case of that used in Section 2 of Chapter 3. Rather than a gradual upward-sloping industry supply curve, it is assumed that new capital goods are perfectly elastically supplied at price $\bar{p}_I$ up to a maximum rate ($\bar{I}_0$) in the short run. Additions to capacity, which come in discrete form, take time to build but eventually shift the supply curve out horizontally to the right (from $\bar{I}_0$ to $\bar{I}_I$, say). Thus, up to a maximum rate of investment I_0, investment will be demand-determined. At $\bar{I}_0$, a capacity constraint is hit as output cannot be increased beyond $\bar{I}_0$ in the short run.

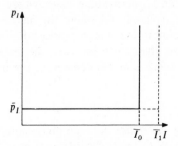

Figure 8.1

It now remains to integrate the two sides of the market, and to do so it is useful to consider some basics using instantaneous demand and supply curves before turning to the full analysis. Suppose, then, that the industry is initially in equilibrium with some spare capacity held to meet marginal unforeseen demands. Suppose also that an event occurs which causes the demand curve for investment to shift out to the right, from I_0^d to I_1^d in Figure 8.2. At the existing capital goods price, $\bar{p}_I$, this causes excess demand in the short run, given capacity $\bar{I}_0$. There are now several possibilities, depending on the extent to which markets

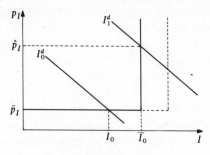

Figure 8.2

clear:

1. If prices are perfectly flexible, the price of capital goods will rise to ensure the equality of demand and supply. With supply given at $\bar{I}_0$, the price of capital goods will rise to $\hat{p}_I$.
2. If prices are completely inflexible at $\bar{p}_I$, excess demand will persist until sufficient additional capacity is built.

Clearly, there are also intermediate cases where prices do react gradually to excess demand and where the market does not clear continuously. The assumption of perfect price inflexibility was the one made in the previous chapter. In this case, the first-order condition tells us that, when there is excess demand in the investment goods market,

$$\mu - \lambda = \bar{p}_I C'(\bar{I}_0) \tag{11}$$

with λ representing the wedge between marginal cost, $\bar{p}_I C'(\bar{I}_0)$, and marginal benefit, μ. With prices flexible, p_I rises to eliminate excess demand and so $\lambda = 0$. In order to have demand equal to supply, we need

$$I^d = I(q) = \bar{I}_0 \tag{12}$$

and therefore we must have

$$q = \bar{q}_0 = C'(\bar{I}_0). \tag{13}$$

Therefore

$$\mu/\hat{p}_I = C'(\bar{I}_0) \Rightarrow \hat{p}_I = \mu/C'(\bar{I}_0).$$

It is simplest to begin by making the strong assumption of price inflexibility, despite the capacity constraint that may operate. Assume then that a previously unanticipated event occurs at time t_0 which increases investment demand above the available short-run supply, $\bar{I}_0$. Simply for convenience, we shall assume that the capital-goods-producing industry is initially in long-run equilibrium with just sufficient capacity to meet the existing demand for replacement investment; that is, $\bar{I}_0 = \delta K_0$. As time passes, discrete additions to capacity take place until eventually sufficient capacity exists to meet the investment demand. Without saying for the time being how the building of capacity responds to excess demand, we model this process by assuming that, after a known time interval $(t_1 - t_0)$, additional capacity comes on stream and the maximum rate of output of the supplying industry increases to $\bar{I}_1$.[1] After a further interval of time $(t_1' - t_1)$, sufficient capacity has been added to meet the additional demand.

Formally, the solution of this problem is to find a path for (q, K) that satisfies the following sets of equations of motion:

$$\left. \begin{aligned} \dot{q} &= q(r+\delta) - \frac{wF_K(\cdot)}{\bar{p}_I F_L(\cdot)} \\ \dot{K} &= I(q) - \delta K \end{aligned} \right\} \quad \text{for } t < t_0 \tag{14}$$

$$\left. \begin{aligned} \dot{q} &= q(r+\delta) - \frac{wF_K(\cdot)}{\bar{p}_I F_L(\cdot)} \\ \dot{K} &= \bar{I}_0 - \delta K \end{aligned} \right\} \quad \text{for } t_0 \leqslant t < t_1 \tag{15}$$

$$\left. \begin{aligned} \dot{q} &= q(r+\delta) - \frac{wF_K(\cdot)}{\bar{p}_I F_L(\cdot)} \\ \dot{K} &= \bar{I}_1 - \delta K \end{aligned} \right\} \quad \text{for } t_1 \leqslant t < t_1' \tag{16}$$

$$\left. \begin{aligned} \dot{q} &= q(r+\delta) - \frac{wF_K(\cdot)}{\bar{p}_I F_L(\cdot)} \\ \dot{K} &= I(q) - \delta K \end{aligned} \right\} \quad \text{for } t \geqslant t_1'. \tag{17}$$

The phase diagram for this case is shown in Figure 8.3. Its explanation is as follows. At t_0 an unanticipated permanent increase in demand (say) from $\bar{Q}_0$ to $\bar{Q}_1$ shifts out the $\dot{q} = 0$ locus. Over the period t_0 to t_1, q is driven by the equations of motion (15), and since $\bar{I}_0 = \delta K_0$ and the firm begins in steady state with capital stock K_0 there is no

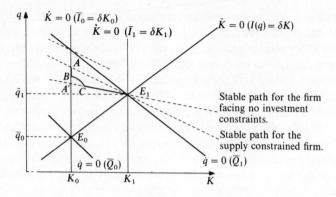

Figure 8.3

change in capital stock over this period. q therefore jumps up to A and then gradually falls as increased investment, higher capital stocks, and lower marginal products draw nearer. At time t_1, B is reached and (q, K) are then determined by the equation of motion (16). Over the period t_1 to t'_1 the movement of (q, K) is governed by the requirement that a point on the unconstrained stable path (C) is reached at t'_1 in order that μ and therefore q follow a continuous path. Since the constrained stable path (for $\bar{I} = \bar{I}_1$) is steeper than the unconstrained stable path (see Chapter 7), point B must lie below the former if the latter is to be reached along a continuous path. At C sufficient capacity has been built to meet investment demand and the firm is unconstrained, moving down the appropriate stable path to the steady-state position E_1.

The path for investment and capital stock is therefore as shown in Figure 8.4. Actual investment is given by $\min(I^d, I^s)$ and shown by the

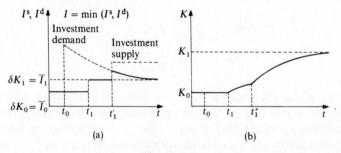

Figure 8.4

solid line in Figure 8.4(a). We can see that, for a cost-minimizing firm, the effect of delays in the availability of capital is, unsurprisingly, given the analysis of Chapter 7, to raise marginal 'q' above what it would otherwise have been (A' in Figure 8.3). Investment and marginal 'q' are *negatively* related, because actual investment is supply-determined until such time as sufficient capacity has been built to eliminate any excess demand.

We now use the same diagram to analyse the case of price flexibility. Above, the supply side of the industry responds to excess demand by building additional capacity with no movement in the price of capital goods. In fact, the price of capital goods is likely to respond to excess demand, and we now go to the opposite extreme and make the assumption of perfect price flexibility where the price of investment goods moves so as always to eliminate any excess demand or supply. We also make the assumption that, despite movements in capital goods prices, the behaviour of the supply side is exactly as before, with additional capacity taking as long to come on stream. We shall relax this assumption later. For the time being this implies, with $\lambda = 0$ and $I^d = I(q) = I^s = \bar{I}$, that

for $t_0 \leqslant t < t_1$: $\qquad I^d = I(\bar{q}_0) = I^s = \bar{I}_0$

for $t_1 \leqslant t < t'_1$: $\qquad I^d = I(\bar{q}_1) = I^s = \bar{I}_1$

for $t'_1 \leqslant t$: $\qquad I^d = I(q) \ = I\left(\dfrac{\mu}{\bar{p}_I}\right).$

Therefore for $t_0 \leqslant t < t_1$, p_I must move so as to ensure that

$$\frac{\mu}{p_I} = \bar{q}_0 \Rightarrow \frac{\dot{\mu}}{\bar{q}_0} = \dot{p}_I;$$

for $t_1 \leqslant t < t'_1$, we require

$$\frac{\mu}{p_I} = \bar{q}_1 \Rightarrow \frac{\dot{\mu}}{\bar{q}_1} = \dot{p}_I;$$

and finally, for $t'_1 \leqslant t$,

$$q = \frac{\mu}{\bar{p}_I} \Rightarrow \dot{p}_I = 0 \quad \text{and} \quad \dot{q} = \frac{\dot{\mu}}{p_I}.$$

Thus, until the capacity constraint is lifted, the behaviour of the price of capital goods is determined by μ. But we know the behaviour of μ, which is *exactly as before* (the fixed price case). By definition,

$$\mu(t) = \int_t^\infty w(s)\frac{F_K(s)}{F_L(s)} \exp\{-(r+\delta)(s-t)\}\, ds$$

and μ simply describes how the series of discounted marginal profits from a unit of capital is expected to move. Given demand and relative prices, this is determined by the anticipated path of investment and hence the capital stock. Since for the time being we are assuming that additional capacity is available at exactly the same time as before, investment is as before and μ follows exactly the same path. The path of μ can be deduced from the phase diagram since, with capital goods prices fixed at $\bar{p}_I$, $\dot{q} = \mu/\bar{p}_I$. The paths of μ, q, and p_I are therefore as illustrated in Figure 8.5.

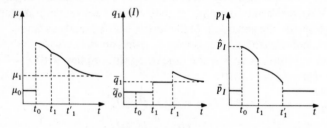

Figure 8.5

We now contrast this with the conclusions drawn previously. Earlier we saw that, as in Chapter 7, the effect of the supply constraint was to raise marginal 'q', but that investment was no longer positively related to 'q'. Indeed, investment and marginal 'q' were negatively related during the period t_0 to t_1'. In this case, the behaviour of actual investment is, by assumption, identical, but the behaviour of marginal 'q' and the relationship between 'q' and investment is completely changed. Investment and 'q' are now positively related, since 'q' no longer increases instantaneously and then gradually falls as a result of the supply constraint. Instead, 'q' remains constant and subsequently rises. Not only this, but we can see from the diagrams that the path of 'q' is discontinuous with therefore anticipated jumps in 'q' and p_I. Since in earlier chapters I argued that the path of 'q' must be continuous, this requires some explanation. Does it violate any postulate of rational behaviour? Are there supernormal returns to be made along such paths? To see why the answer is no, we must return to a careful consideration of the reasons for the continuity of the path of 'q' in one previous analysis. With the price of capital goods fixed at unity, the first-order conditions for a cost-minimizing firm are

$$\dot{\mu} = \mu(r+\delta) = w\,\frac{F_K(\cdot)}{F_L(\cdot)}.$$

and

$$\mu = 1 + C'(I).$$

The important thing to note is that it is the equation $\mu = 1 + C'(I)$ that is an equilibrium condition. The equation of motion for μ is a description of behaviour depicting how μ moves given current and expected capital stocks and employment of the firm. This is explicit when we integrate forward the equation of motion of μ to give

$$\mu(t) = \int_t^\infty w(s)\frac{F_K(s)}{F_L(s)}\exp\{-(r+\delta)(s-t)\}\,ds.$$

But it follows immediately from this that along any *anticipated* path μ must be continuous. Since $\mu(t)$ summarizes how much firms are willing to pay at time t for a unit of capital, it must reflect their expectations of the future returns to that unit of capital. By definition, therefore, except in response to new information, μ cannot jump. If it did so, this would imply two different sets of expectations. In fact, the discontinuity of 'q' follows from the assumption about the discrete additions to capacity on the supply side and the assumption of market-clearing. With investment demand, $I(q)$, continuously equal to investment supply, 'q' must jump as investment supply does. With μ continuous, this in turn implies jumps in the price of capital goods.

3 The Effect of Different Supply-side Assumptions

We shall now relax some of the particular assumptions made on the supply side. To do this we shall assume that demanding firms are unconstrained in the product market. In this way we can again contrast the results with those of the previous chapter; in addition, the particular properties of this demand-side specification highlight the role of different assumptions about supply in determining the behaviour of investment capital goods prices and 'q'.

From Section 2, the equation of motion for 'q' is

$$\dot{q} = q\left(r+\delta-\frac{\dot{p}_I}{p_I}\right) - \frac{F_K(\cdot)}{p_I}.$$

We also know from (4), (5) that $\dot{\mu} = \mu(r+\delta) - F_K(\cdot)$ and $F_L(\cdot) = w$.

In other words, exactly as in earlier chapters, given a constant-return-to-scale Cobb–Douglas production function, μ is determined entirely by the real wage for a constant interest and depreciation rate. For a constant r, δ, w, μ is constant and unaffected by changes in the rate of investment. But since $q = \mu/p_I$, this assumption makes it particularly useful for focusing on different assumptions about market behaviour.

Consider then the analysis of the previous section for the unconstrained firm. Let there be an unanticipated permanent fall in the wage rate from w_0 to w_1 which, at the initial price of capital goods, increases investment demand; given the same assumption on the supply side, the behaviour of μ, 'q', and investment is shown in Figure 8.6(a) for the case of price inflexibility and in 8.6(b) for the case of price flexibility.

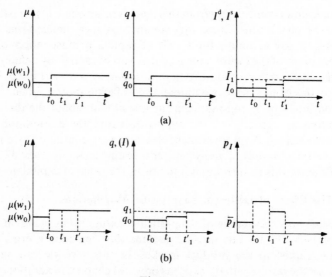

(a)

(b)

Figure 8.6

The fall in the real wage increases investment demand at the given price of capital goods $\bar{p}_I$. There is a once-and-for-all increase in μ which implies a similar change in 'q' if capital goods prices remain fixed at $\bar{p}_I$. Investment demand therefore jumps from I_0 to I_1 and then stays constant. With price flexibility, there is a once-and-for-all change in the demand price of capital μ which necessitates an instantaneous increase in capital goods prices in order to equilibrate the market. Therefore capital goods prices remain constant until further capacity is available and the output of the supplying industries can be increased, whereupon the price of capital goods drops. As in Section 2, therefore, the relationship between behaviour of investment 'q' and capital goods prices depends crucially upon the specification of the market.

The first assumption we shall relax is that of discrete additions to capacity. Though this assumption makes the drawing of phase diagrams feasible and possibly has some realism, it is, as noted, this assumption combined with that of market-clearing which results in the discontinuity of the paths of 'q' and p_I. With gradual expansion of capacity, 'q' and p_I will move continuously and, assuming price flexibility, possible paths for q, I, and p_I are shown in Figure 8.7. Similarly, for the cost-minimizing firm of Section 2 the response of investment would be as shown in Figure 8.8.

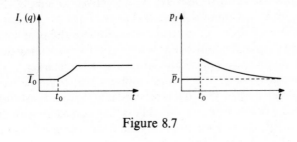

Figure 8.7

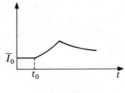

Figure 8.8

The pattern of response drawn in Figure 8.8 where investment gradually increases and subsequently declines is commonly found in empirical work. However, it is only for an anticipated exogenous change that neoclassical 'q' theory, assuming that investment is demand-determined and investment goods are instantaneously available, predicts this response. For unanticipated changes, we known that the response is of an immediate jump in the rate of investment, which declines steadily thereafter. This distinction between the predicted response to anticipated and unanticipated changes will therefore be blurred to the extent that supply cannot be quickly increased or the goods will take time to construct and install.

Next we turn to the assumption that, despite different specifications about price behaviour, the supply of investment goods is identical for both the flexible and the inflexible price assumptions. Of course the two assumptions should not be made independently, since the behaviour of capital goods prices provides incentives to increase supply just as, on the demand side, the price affects the incentive to purchase capital goods. In fact, although recent theory, focusing on the demand side, interprets the definition of 'q' ('the ratio of market value to replacement cost') to mean the ratio of demand price to the market price of new capital goods, there is another equally valid interpretation which focuses on the incentives to supply the new capital goods. The ratio of the market price of new investment goods to their marginal cost of production determines the profitability of increased output, with any wedge between the two providing suppliers with an incentive to put additional goods on the market.[2]

While there are a variety of assumptions that could be made, an obvious one to begin with, if it is believed that there are costs involved in changing production levels rapidly, is that, compared with the case where capital goods prices are inflexible, firms increase their production more rapidly the larger is the price incentive. In other words, $I^s = f(p_I - \bar{p}_I)$. Given this, and continuing with our assumption of no spare capacity initially, the paths of I and p_I for firms unconstrained in the product market are as shown in Figure 8.9.

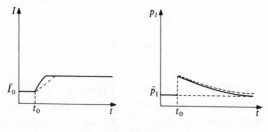

Figure 8.9

Following on from this, one can also generalize the assumption about the nature of the supply curve. The short-run capacity constraint, where supply becomes insensitive to price, clearly dampens the initial response of investment to increases in demand. By assuming the more traditional upward-sloping short-run industry supply in conjunction with that of a long-run horizontal supply curve, the initial increase in investment would be larger and the increase in prices smaller following an increase in demand (Figure 8.10). However, it would be wrong to exaggerate the importance of this generalization. Substantially the same results would be achieved with the perpendicular short-run supply curve if there existed some initial spare capacity. Finally, it is also clearly possible to relax the assumption of a horizontal long-run industry supply curve.

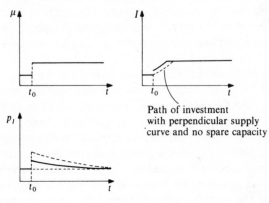

Path of investment
with perpendicular supply
curve and no spare capacity

Fig. 8.10

4 Conclusion

Neoclassical investment theory pays little attention to supply behaviour. In the 'q' theory literature this manifests itself in investment being demand-determined with new capital goods being instantaneously available, and in the all-embracing assumption of adjustment costs to explain discrepancies between market value and replacement cost. Tobin and Brainard are more careful in explaining such divergences between market value and replacement cost: 'This profit is not wiped out immediately because construction takes time and rapid construction is especially expensive both for the individual builder and the economy as a whole' (Tobin and Brainard, 1977).

Simply specifying costs of adjustment that are strictly increasing in the rate of investment is an uncomfortably general assumption with which to capture the variety of different circumstances under which changes in investment take place. Whether it is because construction takes time—or, to use an old distinction, whether it is internal or external adjustment costs that are relevant—will affect the movements of and interrelationships between investment and 'q'.

In this chapter I have tried to address some of these questions by examining investment and 'q' when additional capital goods may not be available instantaneously. While retaining the assumption of adjustment costs on the demand side of the market, I have tried to model explicitly other adjustment costs that may occur using a particular specification of supply-side behaviour. Although not rigorously derived from an optimizing model, the specification is nevertheless one that has been used many times before, and it suffices to show the value of explicitly incorporating the supply side rather than leaving its influence to be covered simply by the assumption of 'adjustment costs', $C(I)$.

We have seen how different assumptions about the supply side can imply very different behaviour of and relationships between 'q', investment, and the price of capital goods. If capital goods prices are inflexible, then 'q' reacts as in the previous chapter to supply constraints. However, investment is, of course, no longer determined by 'q'. Alternatively, if capital goods prices are flexible, then investment is again positively related to 'q' but 'q' itself can behave very differently. In addition, we have seen how discrete additions to the capacity of the capital-goods-producing industry can cause *anticipated jumps in* 'q' (and the price of capital goods) and have suggested one reason why the actual response of investment to unanticipated and anticipated changes in exogenous variables may not be as distinct as predicted by previous authors.

Notes

1. Again, for convenience in drawing the phase diagram, we assume that $\bar{I}_1$ = δK_1, i.e. replacement investment in the new steady state.
2. Tobin and Brainard (1977) seem to prefer this perspective in talking of the construction industry: 'An increase in the market valuation of houses relative to the current cost of building will encourage residential construction. The incentive is the gain to be made by the excess of market price over replacement cost' (p. 236).

9

Conclusion

In this book I have tried to provide a comprehensive study of investment theory in a framework that combines the use of rational expectations and disequilibrium theory. I have worked through many examples in detail, using phase diagrams to illustrate the results. In this way I hope the reader not only will have been able to appreciate more about investment theory, but also will now be more familiar with both the strengths and weaknesses of rational expectations theory and disequilibrium theory. On investment theory itself, I have tried to integrate the supply side of the investment process into different models and to provide a general analysis of investment when markets do not clear. In so doing, I also hope to have clarified the relationship between Keynes, Jorgenson, Tobin and other theories of investment.

After quickly summarizing the main theories of investment in Chapter 1, I argued in Chapter 2 that consideration of the capital-goods-producing industry and the treatment of expectations were the distinguishing features of Keynes's investment theory. In looking at the work of Witte (1963), we saw that he correctly stresses that the Keynesian investment function is a market equilibrium curve and hence is concerned with actual investment and not investment demand. He shows clearly that Keynes's equilibrium is characterized by the equality of supply and demand price, and therefore that the position of the supply curve of the capital-goods-producing industry is vital. Despite this, there are a number of faults with the Witte model.

To remedy this, in Chapter 3 I extended the work of Marshall, Simpson and Sedgwick (1975) to show how a rational expectations, neoclassical model of investment, which incorporates an upward-sloping supply function for new capital goods, produces a 'Keynesian' model of investment, capable of reflecting the importance placed by Keynes upon expectations and 'animal spirits'. In this model the higher supply price of capital goods, implied by an increase in investment demand, causes firms to spread their investment response and to react immediately to anticipated changes in exogenous variables that affect the demand price of capital. The unrealistic features of Jorgenson's original contribution, with its famous myopic first-order condition, are thereby avoided. I argued that it is therefore not the assumptions of a putty–putty technology and zero costs of adjustment *per se* that produce myopic behaviour, as in the original version of Jorgenson, but rather his unrealistic price adjustment assumption. I also argued that the distinction between anticipated and unanticipated changes allows a consistent re-interpretation of Witte.

In Chapter 4 I looked quickly at the relationship between Keynes and Tobin's '*q*' theory before turning to a detailed analysis of the '*q*' theory of investment (generalized neoclassical model), when markets need not clear. I first clarified the relationship between investment and stock market values by generalizing Hayashi's (1982) result to a world of non-market clearing.

I showed that the relationship between marginal and average '*q*', and therefore the appropriate form of the investment equation, depends upon market conditions, both current and anticipated. If markets do not clear continuously, marginal and average '*q*' are not equal, with the divergence reflecting the extent of rationing. I argued that this does not seem to have been fully appreciated by empirical researchers since, strictly speaking, investment equations that simply regress investment against average '*q*' are inconsistent with the previously popular equations containing an exogenous demand term. The latter has the implicit assumption of a sales constraint, while the former, if appropriate, involves the assumption of no demand (or any other) constraint.

Chapters 5, 6, and 7 provided a general intertemporal theory of the firm when markets do not clear. However, our particular focus is, of course, the investment decision. In Chapter 5, we looked primarily at demand constraints and at a unified analysis of the traditionally independent cost minimization and profit maximization approaches to investment theory. Chapter 6 used this model to look at the response of investment to demand and relative price changes. In the context of the putty–putty/putty–clay debate, an article by Abel (1981) shows how, as would be expected from a putty–clay model, firms with a putty–putty technology, and subject to costs of adjustment, may react more quickly to an increase in demand than to a change in relative prices. I argued that the Abel framework–that of the cost-minimizing firm–is unnecessarily restrictive since, given relative prices, there will be some levels of demand that firms will not produce. Using the integrated model of Chapter 5, I showed that the variety of dynamic responses that is possible means that one cannot draw any unambiguous conclusion about the relative speeds of response. The strongest contrast in results was, as in Malinvaud (1977), obtained for wage rate changes. An important empirical implication from this and other chapters is that, because firms' investment behaviour depends closely upon the market conditions under which they operate, it is no use expecting parameter estimates relevant to one set of market conditions necessarily to be a reliable guide to behaviour under another. Ideally, empirical models should also be sufficiently general to take account of non-market-clearing.

Chapters 7 and 8 returned to the question of supply-side behaviour. Chapter 7 extended 'q' theory to consider the effects of disequilibrium in the capital goods market. Building on the earlier chapters, I looked at the effects upon firms that may be both demand-constrained and unconstrained of being unable to buy, either now or in the future, all the investment goods they wish. The analysis is again general and contained as a special case the problem of irreversibility of investment studied by Arrow (1968) and Nickell (1974a, 1974b). I showed how, for a constant-returns-to-scale firm, the effects of investment constraints differ according to whether the firm is demand-constrained or not. For an unconstrained firm, we saw, perhaps surprisingly, that marginal 'q' is completely unaltered by an investment constraint. In Chapter 8 I was more specific about the behaviour of the capital goods industry that may underlie some of the investment constraints. Using a simple model of the supply side, I incorporated the possibility both that firms may choose not to produce new capital goods and that, even if there were such an incentive, the goods may not be instantaneously available. We saw that, even in this simple model, different assumptions about the supply side can imply very different behaviour of, and relationships between, q, investment, and the price of capital goods.

Finally, and very briefly, I should now like to suggest areas for future research. The first must be a relaxation of the assumption of exogenous constraints and no reaction of prices to those constraints; agents can and do influence the extent to which they are constrained, and a careful investigation of how prices and quantities change under such circumstances is called for. Second, I have illustrated the potential importance of the capital-goods-supplying industry in determining aggregate investment. Further attention should be paid to an accurate specification of the interdependence between both sides of the market.

Third, in empirical work aggregate investment models must take account of this kind of interdependence. For instance, almost all studies are really estimating an equation that is a combination of demand and supply elements. Most studies do not formulate an equation for the supply of capital goods. As Junankar (1972) has pointed out: "One of the reasons for the contradictory results obtained in empirical work on investment may be because the estimates are of a hybrid relation rather than because of the demand (or supply) equation itself."

Bibliography

Abel, Andrew B. (1979), *Investment and the Value of Capital*. New York: Garland.
—— (1981), 'Dynamic Adjustment in a Putty Putty Model: Implications for Testing the Putty Clay Hypothesis', *International Economic Review*, 22(1), 19–36.
Ackley, Gardner (1961), *Macroeconomic Theory*. London: Macmillan.
Arrow, Kenneth J. (1968), 'Optimal Capital Policy with Irreversible Investment', in J. N. Wolfe (ed.), *Value, Capital and Growth. Essays in Honour of Sir John Hicks*. Edinburgh University Press.
—— and Kurz, Mordecai (1970), *Public Investment, The Rate of Return, and Optimal Fiscal Policy*. Baltimore: Johns Hopkins Press.
Barro, Robert J., and Grossman, Herschel I. (1971), 'A General Disequilibrium Model of Income and Employment', *American Economic Review*, 61, 82–93.
Bean, Charles R. (1981), 'An Economic Model of Manufacturing Investment in the UK', *Economic Journal*, 91, 106–21.
Begg, David K. H. (1982a), *The Rational Expectations Revolution in Macroeconomics: Theories and Evidence*. Oxford: Philip Allan.
—— (1982b), 'Rational Expectations, Wage Rigidity and Involuntary Unemployment: A Particular Theory', *Oxford Economic Papers*, 34(1), 23–47.
Bischoff, C. W. (1969), 'Hypothesis Testing and the Demand for Capital Goods', *Review of Economics and Statistics*, 51, 354–68.
—— (1971a), 'The Effect of Alternative Lag Distributions', in Gary Fromm (ed.), *Tax Incentives and Capital Spending*. Washington, DC: Brookings Institution, pp. 61–130.
—— (1971b), 'Business Investment in the 1970s: A Comparison of Models', *Brookings Papers on Economic Activity*, 1, 13–58.
Blanchard, Olivier J., and Sachs, Jeffrey D. (1982), 'Anticipations, Recessions, and Policy: An Intertemporal Disequilibrium Model', *National Bureau of Economic Research Working Paper*, no. 971.
Bliss, Christopher J. (1975), 'The Reappraisal of Keynes' Economics: An Appraisal', in M. Parkin and A. R. Nobay (eds), *Current Economic Problems: The Proceedings of the Annual Meetings of the AUTE*. Oxford: Basil Blackwell.

Brechling, Frank P. (1975), *Investment and Employment Decisions.* Manchester University Press.

Ciccolo, John H. (1975), 'Four Essays on Monetary Policy'. Ph.D. thesis, Yale University.

Dornbusch, Rudiger (1976), 'Expectations and Exchange Rate Dynamics', *Journal of Political Economy*, 84, 1161–77.

Edwards, Jeremy S. S. and Keen, Michael J. (1983), 'Taxation, Investment and Marginal q'. Unpublished paper (mimeo).

Eisner, R. and Nadiri, M. I. (1968), 'Investment Behaviour and Neoclassical Theory', *Review of Economics and Statistics*, 50, 369–82.

—— (1970), 'Neoclassical Theory of Investment Behaviour: A Comment', *Review of Economics and Statistics*, 52, 216–22.

von Furstenberg, George M. (1977), 'Corporate Investment: Does Market Valuation Matter in the Aggregate?' *Brookings Papers on Economic Activity*, no. 2, 347–97.

Gould, Jeremy P. (1968), 'Adjustment Costs in the Theory of Investment of the Firm', *Review of Economic Studies*, 35, 47–56.

Grossman, Herschel I. (1972), 'A Choice Theoretic Model of an Income–Investment Accelerator', *American Economic Review*, 67, 630–41.

Haavelmo, T. (1960), *A Study in the Theory of Investment.* University of Chicago Press.

Hausman, Jerry A. (1973), 'Theoretical and Empirical Aspects of Vintage Capital Models'. Unpublished D.Phil. thesis, Oxford University.

Hayashi, Fumio (1982), 'Tobin's Marginal q and Average q: A Neoclassical Interpretation', *Econometrica*, 50, 213–24.

Hirshleifer, Jack (1970), *Investment, Interest and Capital.* London: Macmillan.

Jenkinson, Nigel H. (1981), 'Investment, Profitability, and the Valuation Ratio', *Bank of England Discussion Paper* no. 4.

Jorgenson, Dale W. (1963), 'Capital Theory and Investment Behaviour', *American Economic Review*, 53, 247–56.

—— (1966), 'The Theory of Investment Behaviour', in R. Ferber (ed.), *Determinants of Investment Behaviour.* New York: National Bureau of Economic Research.

—— (1972), 'Investment Behaviour and the Production Function', *Bell Journal of Economics*, 3, 220–51.

Junankar, P. M. (1972), *Investment: Theories and Evidence.* London: Macmillan.

Keynes, John M. (1936), *The General Theory of Employment, Interest and Money.* London: Macmillan.

—— (1937), 'The General Theory of Employment', *Quarterly Journal of Economics*, 51, 209–23.

Lerner, Abbe P. (1944), *The Economics of Control.* New York: Macmillan.

Lucas, Robert E. (1967), 'Adjustment Costs and the Theory of Supply', *Journal of Political Economy*, 75, 321–34.

—— (1976), 'Econometric Policy Evaluation: A Critique', in K. Brunner and A. H. Meltzer (eds), *The Phillips Curve and Labour Markets*, Supplement to the *Journal of Monetary Economics*.

Malinvaud, Edmond (1977), *The Theory of Unemployment Reconsidered*. Oxford: Basil Blackwell.

—— (1982), 'Wages and Unemployment', *Economic Journal*, 92, 1–13.

Marshall, G. P., Sampson, A. A., and Sedgwick, R. (1975), 'The Rate of Investment and the Supply Schedule for New Capital Goods', *Bulletin of Economic Research*, 27, 30–43.

Mirrlees, James, A. (1975), 'Indeterminate Growth Theory'. Working paper, Nuffield College.

Neary, Peter J., and Stiglitz, Joseph E. (1983), 'Toward a Reconstruction of Keynesian Economics: Expectations and Constrained Equilibrium', *Quarterly Journal of Economics*, 98 (supplement), 199–228.

Nickell, Stephen J. (1974a), 'On the Role of Expectations in the Pure Theory of Investment', *Review of Economic Studies*, 41, 1–20.

—— (1974b), 'On Expectations, Government Policy and the Rate of Investment', *Economica*, 41, 241–55.

—— (1978), *The Investment Decision of Firms*. Cambridge University Press.

Oulton, Nigel (1981), 'Aggregate Investment and Tobin's q: The Evidence from Britain', *Oxford Economic Papers*, 33, 177–202.

Precious, Mark (1979), 'Supply Factors in Investment: A Keynesian Approach'. M.Phil. thesis, University of Oxford.

—— (1985a), 'Rational Expectations, Non-Market-Clearing and Investment Theory'. Unpublished D.Phil. thesis, Oxford University.

—— (1985b), 'Demand Constraints, Rational Expectations and Investment Theory', *Oxford Economic Papers*, 37, 576–605.

Tobin, James (1966), 'Comments on Jorgenson', in R. Ferber (ed.), *Determinants of Investment Behaviour*. New York: National Bureau of Economic Research.

—— (1969), 'A General Equilibrium Approach to Monetary Theory', *Journal of Money, Credit and Banking*, 1, 15–29.

—— and Brainard, William C. (1977), 'Asset Markets and the Cost of Capital', in Bela Belassa and Richard Nelson (eds), *Economic Progress, Private Values and Public Policy: Essays in Honour of William Fellner*.

Treadway, Arthur B. (1969), 'On Rational Entrepreneurial Behaviour and the Demand For Investment', *Review of Economic Studies*, 36, 227–39.

Wilson, Charles A. (1979), 'Anticipated Shocks and Exchange Rate Dynamics', *Journal of Political Economy*, 87, 639–47.

Witte, James G. (1963), 'The Micro-Foundations of the Social Investment Function', *Journal of Political Economy*, 1, 441–56.

Yoshikawa, H. (1980), 'On the 'q' Theory of Investment', *American Economic Review*, 70, 739–43.

Index